The BEAR NECESSITIES of BUSINESS

The

BEAR
NECESSITIES
of # BUSINESS

Building a Company with Heart

MAXINE CLARK

Founder and Chief Executive Bear
Build-A-Bear Workshop®

with Amy Joyner

WILEY

John Wiley & Sons, Inc.

Published by John Wiley & Sons, Inc., Hoboken, New Jersey.
Published simultaneously in Canada.

For general information on our other products and services, or technical support, please contact our Customer Care Department within the United States at (800) 762-2974, outside the United States at (317) 572-3993 or fax (317) 572-4002.

Wiley also publishes its books in a variety of electronic formats. Some content that appears in print may not be available in electronic books. For more information about Wiley products, visit our web site at www.wiley.com.

Build-A-Bear Workshop, Cub Condo, Find-A-Bear, friends 2B made, Build-A-Party, Collectiwear, Beary Limited, Beararmoire, Love Stuff Headquarters, Hugday, Bearemy's Kennel Pals, Read Teddy, Stuffed With Hugs, Huggable Heroes, Bearisms, and Bear Builder are trademarks of Build-A-Bear Workshop, Inc.

Bearisms on pages 311 to 313 are copyrighted by Build-A-Bear Workshop, Inc.

Library of Congress Cataloging-in-Publication Data:

Clark, Maxine K.
    The bear necessities of business : building a company with heart / Maxine Clark with Amy Joyner.
        p.   cm.
    Includes index.
    ISBN-13 978-0-471-77275-0 (cloth)
    ISBN-10 0-471-77275-5 (cloth)
    1. New business enterprises.   2. Entrepreneurship.   I. Joyner, Amy.   II. Title.
    HD62.5.C586   2006
    658—dc22   2005036104

Printed in the United States of America.
10 9 8 7 6 5 4 3 2 1

To "Teddy," wherever you are—thanks for being my first and furriest best friend.

To Kara, Ainsley, Chelsea, Tiffany, Ashley, Chelsey, Hannah, Taylor, Austin, Jason, and all of the Guests of Build-A-Bear Workshop throughout the world. You are my daily inspiration. May you never outgrow your love of stuffed animals and your child's imagination.

Maxine Clark will donate 100 percent of her proceeds from the sales of this book to the **Build-A-Bear-Workshop Bear Hugs Foundation,** which supports meaningful philanthropic efforts for children and families through financial and in-kind support for health and wellness causes and educational and literacy programs.

Contents

PART THREE

Connecting with Your Customers

PART FOUR

Creating an Incredible Experience

PART FIVE
Using Essential Marketing Strategies

PART SIX
Growing Your Business

PART SEVEN
Giving Back

Introduction

Whether you're looking to start a new business, improve an existing one, be a better manager, hire the best employees, or simply get ahead in your current job, this book was written just for you.

The Bear Necessities of Business is your guide to creating a company that uses the most effective marketing strategies, is staffed by workers who look forward to doing their jobs every day, is well regarded by the community, and has an abundance of happy customers.

Like many of you, I began my journey as an entrepreneur and business owner with a dream. After venturing out on my own about 10 years ago, I had visions of revolutionizing an industry I spent my entire professional life working in.

To give you a bit of background, upon graduating from the University of Georgia in 1971, I started out as a retail trainee with the May Department Stores Company in Washington, D.C. Over time, I worked my way up, taking on various roles in management. I was involved in everything from planning and research to marketing and

1

product development. Ultimately, I became president of Payless ShoeSource, the discount footwear retailer that May acquired and later spun off.

While I didn't make much money starting out, by the time I rose through the executive ranks I was earning a substantial salary, complete with stock options and a very generous bonus and retirement plan. But I later realized that money alone didn't buy happiness if you weren't doing what you were really passionate about. Quite frankly, I felt the retail business had grown boring and more focused on price than customer satisfaction. Instead, I wanted to put my talents into reenergizing an industry that had been so good to me.

After four years at the top, I left my job at Payless and began looking for another outlet in which to contribute. This time I knew I wanted to create a company of my own, even though at first I didn't know exactly what it would look like.

The concept began to crystallize in my mind during a shopping trip with a young friend of mine to find some collectible stuffed animals. It turned out the store was out of the particular toy she was looking for. You'll read more about this event in the book, but this visit gave me the idea to start what eventually became known as Build-A-Bear Workshop.

In a nutshell, I wanted to create a company that would let people make their own customized furry friends. I initially tried to get the owners of a stuffed animal factory with a similar concept to sell their business to me. When they declined, I began putting together a plan to build this business from scratch. You'll soon discover the blueprint I followed, and the journey that ensued.

Needless to say, my original vision has turned into something bigger than I ever dreamed. The first Build-A-Bear Workshop store opened in October 1997 at a mall in Saint Louis, Missouri. That initial year, we recorded sales of $1.7 million, well ahead of expectations. Today we are a publicly traded company, with more than 200 locations around the world. We have grown into the leading company (and the only international one) providing customers with a make-your-own-stuffed-animal interactive experience. So far, we have made furry friends for more than 30 million Guests (which is what we call our customers). We have more than 750 full-time employees (or associates, as we refer to them), along with some 5,000 part-timers. Build-A-Bear Workshop is already one of the nation's top 15 toy retailers with annual sales of more than $350 million as of the end of 2005.

I'm proud that our company has been continuously lauded and recognized for its excellence in Guest satisfaction, marketing, innovation, and for being such a great place to work. I can't tell you how many letters and e-mails I get from people every day asking how I accomplished so much in such a relatively short amount of time. You'll uncover the answers in *The Bear Necessities of Business*.

Although I wrote this book especially for those of you wanting to know what it really takes to get into business for yourself, I'm convinced that everyone seeking to become more successful can apply the strategies found in each of these chapters to their own lives. The lessons hold true even if you work for someone else and have no plans to strike out on your own. After all, the best employees are those who think like entrepreneurs. That attitude will take you further than you can imagine. It certainly worked for me. I have followed all of the principles in this book during more than three decades in business and throughout my entire life.

Among other things, I'll show you how I built my company from the ground up, and tell you how we managed to develop such an incredible following of loyal Guests of all ages. I learned long ago that the key to long-term survival in any industry is keeping your customers happy. I believe that we are well on our way to accomplishing this, as evidenced by the impressive repeat business we experience at Build-A-Bear Workshop.

The Bear Necessities of Business is divided into seven parts, each built around the essential elements necessary to start, run, and market a thriving company. The principles apply to every industry, and work whether your target audience is children, teenagers, baby boomers, senior citizens, or any age in between. Every part contains a series of short chapters further expanding on required elements necessary for you to stand apart from the competition.

While I primarily draw upon my experiences in creating and running Build-A-Bear Workshop, I also give you the wisdom learned over my entire career, including lessons and examples from some of the other great companies I admire.

Part One of *The Bear Necessities of Business* discusses the essential ingredients to get your business started, including advice for planning your venture, setting goals, creating strong partnerships, and attracting investors. This section will be of special interest to those of you looking to strike out on your own.

Part Two gives you the secrets to being a great boss. For starters, you must be willing to do any job yourself, no matter how insignificant it may seem, and hire only those who are truly a good fit for your company. I also tell you what we do at Build-A-Bear Workshop to keep our associates motivated and happy, something that actually leads to more productivity and higher profits.

Part Three discusses the importance of connecting with your customers, and gives you proven strategies for accomplishing this. Among other things, it's crucial for you to see yourself through the eyes of your customers, learn from what they are telling you (often in unspoken ways), and avoid trying to serve every possible demographic. I also tell you how to bring out the childlike excitement in every customer, regardless of how old they are, and give you techniques for making them feel special.

Part Four provides the ingredients for creating an awe-inspiring experience for your customers. As you'll discover, little details make a big difference, and it's crucial to stuff value into every service you provide or product that you sell. In this part, I reveal how to do that.

Part Five discusses the keys to effectively marketing your business, both through advertising, public relations, and word-of-mouth referral (which is often the most effective and least costly method of all). We have really perfected the art of marketing and public relations at Build-A-Bear Workshop, as evidenced by the strong brand recognition we enjoy for such a relatively young company and the hundreds of media placements we have received in everything from the *Wall Street Journal* to my numerous appearances on network and nationally syndicated talk shows.

Part Six provides the insights you need to grow your business. I show you how we've taken our company from one store in Missouri to being on track for more than 300 global locations in the next few years—including our biggest store that recently opened on New York's Fifth Avenue.

Finally, Part Seven talks about the importance of giving back—to your customers, employees, and the community at large. My company, Build-A-Bear Workshop, is a big proponent of community involvement and charitable work, and I'm the first to tell you that success in business is about much more than just making money. In addition to helping the world, sharing good fortune is beneficial to your business in more ways than you might think.

The back of the book features a list of Bearisms we live by as a company. These bits of teddy bear wisdom are a lot of fun, and contain many truths that everyone can benefit from.

Incidentally, while this book is filled with the knowledge I have amassed about running a thriving business over the years, know that my door is always open to you. If, after reading *The Bear Necessities of Business*, you have any additional questions, don't hesitate to drop me a line.

My personal e-mail address is maxineclark@buildabear.com. Yes, I read every e-mail, and try to respond to each one as quickly as possible. The fact that you bought this book means a lot to me, and I hope you'll use the knowledge on these pages to become a huge success. You can also find additional advice about starting a business through a special link on our website at www.buildabear.com.

So let's get started on this exciting journey. I have no doubt that what you are about to read will get your entrepreneurial juices flowing, and I can't wait to hear how you've used this information to accomplish many incredible things.

Part One

Getting Started

Dream the Dream Supreme

People often ask how I was able to take the rough idea for Build-A-Bear Workshop and turn it into such a successful business. Above all, it started when I simply allowed myself to dream. And I'm a true believer in dreaming big.

Since the very beginning, I didn't put restrictions on my vision, nor did I let the way others made or sold stuffed animals stand in my way. Instead, I allowed myself to dream of this unique business going from one store at the Saint Louis Galleria to something that could be as huge as I thought it could be. My dream eventually came true, and continues to evolve even beyond my wildest imagination. But you must start by believing you can truly achieve whatever you set your mind to, no matter how monumental it might seem.

Most people don't do that. They stymie themselves and their ideas with negative thoughts. They're so caught up in what they *can't* do that they don't think about how much they *can* accomplish. As Marianne Williamson wrote in *Return to Love*, "Our deepest fear is not that we are inadequate. Our deepest fear is that we are powerful beyond measure. It is our Light, not our Darkness, that most frightens us."

> *Start by believing you can truly achieve whatever you set your mind to.*

I'm lucky. I've always been a dreamer. I grew up in the 1950s and 1960s, decades when all sorts of seemingly impossible things were happening—small and large. It sounds silly now, in this age of iPods and portable electronic devices, but when I was a kid, transistor radios were a revolutionary invention. You were suddenly able to take sound from faraway voices with you everywhere you went. Someone dreamed up that concept, and the technology became a reality.

My childhood was full of examples of big dreams realized: The first organ transplant was performed, the color television was introduced, a vaccine for polio was developed, Disneyland opened, lasers were invented, the Civil Rights Act was passed, and astronauts rocketed to the moon.

> *Never discount the power of a positive attitude.*

I was fortunate to grow up when I did, in a world where every day brought new inventions. There was nothing to stop me from thinking about what could be, because the unimaginable was becoming reality all the time. Thanks to that inspiration at such a young age, I continue to live in a world of possibility.

My big dream as a kid was to visit Disneyland. I imagined that I was in that magical place every day as I watched my favorite television shows, *The Mickey Mouse Club* and *The Wonderful World of Disney*, each Sunday night. Disneyland represented to me the ultimate in fun, adventure, fantasy, and imagination, as it does for a lot of children—and still does for me.

> *Not dreaming big enough is one of the biggest mistakes entrepreneurs make.*

While I very much wanted to visit the amusement park, my family lived in Florida at the time, a virtual world away from Anaheim, California. (After all, Disney World in Orlando wasn't even on the drawing board then and wasn't built until 1971, the year I graduated from college.) Mom and Dad didn't have the money to spend on something this extravagant. As a result, a cross-country vacation seemed pretty unlikely.

But I didn't let that stop me from dreaming. Although a vacation to Disneyland was temporarily out of reach, it seemed like a perfectly possible goal to one day achieve. I never thought, "Oh, I'll never go there." Instead, I let my imagination go wild, thinking about what it would be like—and what I would do—when I finally arrived.

I had the same optimistic dreamer's mentality when I left Payless ShoeSource and decided to go into business for myself. I never believed I *wouldn't* succeed. I didn't think about the things I *couldn't* do as I built this business. Instead, I focused on what I *could* accomplish. Never underestimate the power of a positive attitude.

> *Think about what your ideal business would look like if there were no obstacles—financial or otherwise—in your way.*

Not dreaming big enough is one of the biggest mistakes entrepreneurs make. They let things like a lack of money or experience hamper them from mapping out the ultimate plan for their business. They don't take the broader 35,000-foot view. They focus on what their limitations are instead of seeing the possibilities. You must envision what can be, embrace it, and be empowered by it.

I challenge you to think about what your ideal business would look like if there were no obstacles—financial or otherwise—in your way. That's what I did in the planning stages for Build-A-Bear Workshop. I put aside financial worries, forgot about the bankers for a while, and pretended that I had as much money as Warren Buffett or Bill Gates. Then I imagined, down to the smallest detail, everything I would need to build a successful brand and company.

It was a grand vision indeed, and although I wasn't able to do all the things I dreamed about immediately, I knew the possibilities that were out there. My vision and the resulting business plan provided me with the ultimate blueprint of goals to work toward as the company (and our profits) grew. Surprisingly, I was able to implement many of the ideas in this blueprint thanks to having envisioned and articulated all that I wanted early on.

Only talk about what's possible.

As just one example, I've always liked how McDonald's packages its Happy Meals—complete with a hamburger, fries, drink, and fun toy—into one cleverly designed box. I wanted to create a similar takeaway case for our stuffed animals. Many retailers, without even thinking about it or doing much research, would have rejected such an idea right away. They would have decided that specialty packaging like this was too expensive, and would have used shopping bags instead. But I don't think like most people. I don't use words like "can't" or "won't." I talk about what's possible, and that's what you should do as well.

With some investigating, I found a supplier able to make our cardboard Cub Condo carrying cases more cheaply than we could buy paper bags! These adorable boxes, now a hallmark of our brand, became carriers for our stuffed animal friends—and double as walking mall billboards.

You alone are responsible for creating your own success.

Sometimes big dreams have to wait. From the time we first opened our doors in 1997, I knew I wanted to have the largest Build-A-Bear Workshop store in the world right in the heart of New York City. Realizing that this location would have to compete with Broadway, the Statue of Liberty, the Empire State Building, and many of the world's biggest and brightest attractions, it was clear that our New York location would have to be magnificent in order to make it in the Big Apple.

That's why we didn't build it immediately. A typical 3,000-square-foot Build-A-Bear Workshop store would have gotten lost in a city where everything is big, bold, and exciting—and where there's so much to do. Plus, when the company was younger, we didn't have the cash or brand recognition to construct such a huge store.

I waited eight years to act on this vision. All the while, my associates, Guests, and I kept thinking up ways to make the New York store even more spectacular. We continued to dream the dream supreme, and now that dream has come true.

Don't let outside forces limit your possibilities.

Build-A-Bear Workshop opened its biggest store in the world on New York's prestigious Fifth Avenue in July 2005. It's what you might call our flagship store. At 20,000 square feet, it's different from any other in the company's portfolio. It's the first store in the world where Guests can create personalized T-shirts for their furry friends or make their own "United Nations" of bears with our entire international Collectiwear line of outfits. The store even houses the ultimate hands-on dining experience, a restaurant called Eat with Your Bear Hands Café. This location has become one of my favorite places in the world, right up there with Disneyland. It turned out even better than I imagined!

You should never be afraid to dream—and dream big—because it's only through such thinking that great things happen. If you can't see it, how can you expect others to? You alone are responsible for creating your own success, so don't let outside forces limit your possibilities.

Let a Child Inspire You

Truth be told, Build-A-Bear Workshop is a business that almost never was.

When I quit my high-profile, financially rewarding job as president of Payless ShoeSource to become an entrepreneur, I did so because I needed more than I was getting out of this seemingly envious corporate position. Sure, my financial bank account was quite healthy. After all, I made a high six-figure income. But despite this, my psychic income bank account was nearly empty. My growing boredom with the retail business led me to decide to put my money where my mouth was.

Kids are insightful because they look at the world differently.

I've always been a big believer that money is not the most important thing in life, and I wanted to do something that was unique and different. My idea was to take the concept of interactive and entertainment retailing, especially for kids, a step beyond where it was by turning it into a true experience. That way I could use my creative talents, while building a business that encouraged the same kind of out-of-the-box thinking in children. I realized there was little, if any, other opportunity for kids to truly get involved and participate, even in the best of today's so-called entertainment stores.

The precise blueprint for the business came together for me during a shopping expedition with my wonderful young friend Katie Burkhardt, who was 10 years old at the time.

Katie is the daughter of one of my good friends. Even when she was young, I considered Katie to be one of my best friends, too, since we enjoyed many of the same things.

I know that's an odd thing for a woman in her mid-50s to say. But we were—and still are—very close. Perhaps it has something to do with the fact that I've never had children of my own. One thing's for sure: It was Katie (and her teddy bear George) who provided the initial inspiration for this company.

When I moved from Topeka, Kansas (home of Payless Shoe-Source) to Saint Louis, I used to pick Katie and her brother Jack up from school for fun afternoon outings. One of our favorite things to do together was scour local stores to look for Ty Beanie Babies. Both Jack and Katie were collectors, and we were always looking for pieces of the company's stuffed animal collection they didn't already have. One afternoon, we stopped by a store with a big sign on the door touting its huge selection of Beanie Babies. To our disappointment, we didn't find a single animal there that Jack and Katie didn't own or hadn't seen before.

Listening to children can help you figure out what their parents want.

Katie doesn't really remember this next part, but thank goodness I do. You might say it was that eureka moment that helped to crystallize what kind of new business I wanted to start. She picked up one of the Beanie Babies and examined it with a critical eye. "You know," she said, "these are so simple. We could make these."

She meant that we could buy some plush fabric and beans, go home to my basement, and stitch up some homemade stuffed animals as a craft project. But what I heard with my entrepreneurial ears was a big idea with so much more potential. Suddenly, I'd found the inspiration for my new business. You know what they say: "out of the mouths of babes."

I immediately went into research mode and found a factory (there were actually a few) making bears and giving tours to kids, while allowing them to assist in the manufacturing process. I tried to convince the owners of this factory to sell their business and partner with me to create a bigger vision than what they currently had in place. But they didn't see things the same way and decided not to sell. When I went back to Katie and told her this, she replied, "This is soooo cool, we just have to do it ourselves. Had she said, "*You* just have to do it," I don't know whether I would have been as excited about it. But she was already engaged in the concept and saw the same possibilities that I saw.

Katie was the first child to provide the initial inspiration for the company, but she's certainly not the last. Every day, I listen to what young children have to say, and not just so I can figure out how to make them or their parents buy more from our stores.

Seek the opinions of kids when starting your business, even if they're not in your target demographic.

Kids are just plain insightful, regardless of the business you're in. You don't have to run a retail store for children to benefit from their knowledge. They look at the world differently from most adults. They aren't afraid to be silly or show their emotions. They're naturally kind and mostly unafraid. They don't censor themselves for fear of sounding stupid or having their ideas judged to be bad. They speak their minds and say such amazing and spontaneous things. These are all the sorts of traits you need, so seek the opinions of kids when starting your business, even if they're not in your target demographic.

In short, kids are worth listening to, and their opinions are very important. You never know how a child's words might inspire you.

Do What You Love

To be happy in your business, and therefore more successful, you must do work you are passionate about. Whether it's selling goods or providing services, every day needs to be a joy. Otherwise, all the money in the world won't matter.

I once heard former National Football League (NFL) great Terry Bradshaw speak exuberantly about his job as quarterback for the Pittsburgh Steelers and how he enjoyed going to work every day. He said he had so much fun, most days he thought he ought to pay the Steelers for allowing him to do a job he so loved. He was essentially being paid to practice his hobby.

To be happy and successful in business, you must do work you are passionate about.

That's the same way I feel about Build-A-Bear Workshop. Being Chief Executive Bear isn't just my job; it's my passion. I can't wait to get to work every morning.

Everyone deserves to do what he or she loves. Anything else means accepting second best and leading an unfulfilling life.

I graduated from the University of Georgia in 1971, quite a tumultuous and pivotal time in our country. The Vietnam War had awakened many to activism. People spoke up for what they believed in, especially on college campuses, be it equal rights for women or peace in Vietnam. Folks embraced what they loved and no job was off-limits—regardless of your gender or background. You could be an activist, lawyer, businessperson, politician, or anything else you desired. The possibilities were endless, as were the opportunities around the globe. (You could say that was the start of our world becoming so "flat," to use the phrase coined by Thomas Friedman in his book on globalization, *The World Is Flat* (Farrar, Straus & Giroux, 2005).

In college I discovered that I really loved the idea of working for a consumer-oriented business. One of my professors, Dr. Robert Carter, was a consultant for many retail companies. He talked about these retailers during his lectures and gave us real-life projects to work on as case studies. Dr. Carter's lessons sparked my creativity and interest in retailing. It was this inspiration that led me to pursue a career in the field.

I started my retailing career as an executive trainee for the May Department Stores Company right out of college, working at one of the chain's Washington, D.C., stores. I had a string of different jobs through the years with May, starting in the main department store division, and then moving on to the Venture Stores discount division. Next it was on to Payless ShoeSource, followed by my current role at Build-A-Bear Workshop. I've been truly happy in all of these positions because I recognized all that I was learning from each job. Every place I have worked has helped me to become who I am today. My career has been a true labor of love. I'm not even sure *labor* is the best word to use, because I've always had so much fun.

When I consider all the people I've admired through the years—

from Walt Disney to my parents, their friends, teachers, relatives, coworkers, and mentors—what I remember most is that they were happy. They seemed fulfilled in what they did. I believe their happiness was rooted, at least in part, in the fact that they were doing work they loved. I don't believe you can truly be happy in your work or life unless you are passionate about what you do.

> *Every place you have been has helped you to become the person you are today.*

Happiness for those I admired wasn't contingent on material possessions or money. They found fulfillment in making a difference in the life of an individual, in their hometown, or in the world at large. They each had discovered the greater purpose in their work.

In particular, I remember the bus driver who used to take me to elementary school. He was such a friendly person—he made me smile every day. I always looked forward to the drive to school. By the time I got inside the classroom, I was really excited about what I was going to learn that day. It all started with the welcome I received upon boarding the bus.

While he never said it, I know my bus driver loved his job. He saw his role as a bus driver in a much bigger way. He wasn't just picking up kids from their bus stops and delivering them to school. He was taking us to see the future of the world.

At Build-A-Bear Workshop, I feel like I'm making a difference in the lives of my Guests and associates. I wouldn't do the job if I didn't feel this way. My work has a much greater end result than just selling stuffed animals. I make my living by making people smile. What could be better than that?

I may not be curing cancer or saving people's lives, but I know that I'm making a difference in someone's world. That's what I need to feel emotionally rich and passionate about my work.

Obviously Build-A-Bear Workshop is a special company. I'm

proud that it is doing well and provides a place for such a large number of people to work. But I'm even more pleased that we're able to make so many people happy through simple actions. Our stores are exciting yet comfortable places where families have fun spending time together. That's our impact on the world.

> *The most satisfied people are those who have discovered the greater purpose in their work.*

There are a lot of great things about being the founder of this company. Perhaps the best part is visiting our stores. I love watching children make their bears and seeing their affection for and attachment to their new furry friends. I enjoy talking to them and their parents and grandparents. Their adorable smiles are an added bonus. I also love reading their letters about what Build-A-Bear Workshop and their stuffed animal friends mean to them.

I was lucky to start this company during a time when Guests can easily send you an e-mail to relate their experiences. I get more than 2,500 e-mails and letters each day, many of which I answer myself. We share these letters with our stores as well, showing them how something very small they did made a huge impact on a child or a family. I consider it an honor that our Guests are that engaged in our business, and I take all of their stories, ideas, and insights to heart.

Throughout my career in retailing, I have always viewed the customer as king or queen. Whether I was selling clothes, shoes, or teddy bears, I've always known that I'm doing much more than selling a product. I continuously think of the emotional connection consumers have with the products they're buying.

You can't hug shoes the way you hug a teddy bear, though lots of women (including me) are pretty attached to their shoes. Every product I've sold means more to the person buying it than I could ever know. People don't just buy stuff without a purpose. Something about that product must connect with them. Fulfilling this emotional connection between the consumer and the product has always been the most important (and most fun) part of my job.

> *Don't just focus on selling. Focus on* connecting. *People won't buy unless they have an emotional connection with you and your products.*

No matter what I've been selling, I've always thought about the person who would be buying that product and what it would mean to them. While I was at the May Department Stores Company, I'd think about the woman who was picking out a suit for that big job interview. At Payless ShoeSource, I'd think about the teenage girl who was purchasing a new pair of shoes to wear on a first date with a guy she really wanted to impress. At Build-A-Bear Workshop, I now reflect on all the kids and adults who are making their own special, lifelong furry friends.

I'm convinced that if you love what you do, you'll always find a way to make enough money to sustain yourself and your family. Even if you can't do *exactly* what you want, find a way to come as close as possible to living out your passion.

For instance, one of our associates, Sean Woodard, loves sports. While I'd guess he'd love to be a professional athlete, you know how hard it is to land one of those jobs. But Sean has found another way to live out his passion for sports. He works as a planner in our sports department, helping to plan our line of athletic clothing and accessories for bears. Another colleague, John Hogan, also lives out his love for sports by negotiating deals with all the various teams we have merchandising agreements with. John actually gets paid to go to baseball stadiums and watch a sport that he loves!

Whether it's in your own business or working for someone else, find a way to live out your passions, and think about areas in which you can contribute that play to your passions. Doing so will help you be happy and fulfilled, while allowing you to make a lasting impact on the world.

Beware of Conventional Wisdom

When doing anything new in life—be it going to college, getting married, having a baby, changing jobs, or starting your own business—people inevitably come out of the woodwork offering advice. Some of it is solicited, but most is not.

Still, I always listen to what people have to say because I've learned a lot from others over the years. It was Katie's enthusiasm that convinced me there was a business to be made from making bears. An adult friend talked me into putting hearts into our animals. And a part-time store associate is responsible for getting me to see that we should have our Guests make a wish while creating their bears. All of these things are now very vital parts of our brand's DNA, and I'll tell you more about how they came to be in the next chapter.

Though I do listen, I'm careful about the advice I actually take, and always caution other entrepreneurs and businesspeople to be as well. There's a lot of conventional wisdom out in the world about how things have always been done and how they supposedly *should* be accomplished.

> *Always listen to what others have to say, but be careful about the advice you actually take.*

Granted, conventional wisdom in itself isn't bad. There are numerous ways of doing things and some good general rules to follow. In most cases, if you follow these guidelines, you'll do just fine. The problem with blindly adhering to conventional wisdom is that it likely won't make you very different from the other businesses down the street competing for that same pool of customers; it would make you look like everyone else.

Rather than adhering strictly to the traditional ways of doing things, I challenge myself and those I work with to think more creatively. I'm constantly trying to come up with ways we can take a conventional product or task and put our own unique spin on it by making it more bearish.

For instance, Build-A-Bear Workshop didn't invent teddy bears, nor were we first to create the places that make them. In fact, there were factories that allowed kids to take tours and create their own stuffed animals long before we ever opened our doors. But we put an entirely new spin on the teddy bear business. Instead of just building a factory, we created stores that are special interactive places for families to come together, have fun, and make their own furry friends. We did everything bigger and better than anyone in this business had ever done it before. We saw possibilities like no one else. When I think about some of my other favorite consumer brands, I realize they did the same thing in their respective industries.

> *Conventional wisdom in itself isn't bad. The problem is that following it makes you look like everyone else.*

Howard Schultz didn't invent coffee, but he created Starbucks, the gold standard for coffee shops. Ray Kroc didn't invent hamburgers, but he created McDonald's, a unique brand that has become a global phenomenon.

The key is to build on what's perceived as conventional wisdom, so you can make it your own. That's what every smart company does. It's certainly what we do.

I'm a fan of Steak n Shake, the burger and milkshake restaurant, because it's constantly reinventing traditional products. (Okay, and I love the company's hamburgers and milkshakes, too!) Steak n Shake recently introduced what it calls Sippable Sundaes—milkshakes made with chocolate syrup, whipped cream, and cherries. It also started selling Side-by-Side milkshakes with two kinds of ice cream in the same glass. I don't know about you, but I can never decide between chocolate and vanilla. Now, I don't have to, thanks to the solution Steak n Shake came up with.

Steak n Shake didn't invent the milkshake, but it figured out how to make this venerable drink better. The company built upon what everyone knows to be conventional wisdom in order to take its products to the next level. Lots of places sell milkshakes. But Steak n Shake sells many more now because it offers unique options that customers can't get anywhere else.

I could have opened a conventional toy store filled with premade, prepackaged stuffed animals. It might have been successful, but it wouldn't have been any different from everything else in the marketplace. Being different, essentially being ourselves, has been a key to the success of Build-A-Bear Workshop.

Come up with ways to take a conventional product or task and put your own unique spin on it. Think Starbucks, McDonald's, and even Build-A-Bear Workshop.

When I first shared my idea for the company with others, a lot of people told me what I *shouldn't* do. I listened politely, as I always do, but I didn't let their "don'ts" stop me from doing what I knew was right for this company.

For instance, some of my retail friends told me I was crazy to put our least expensive bear at the front of the store. They said we'd never sell anything but $10 bears. That advice was based on some pretty tried-and-true lessons of retailing. Most retailers bury their cheaper merchandise and their sales or clearance racks at the rear of the store so customers have to walk by the most expensive merchandise first. Retailers figure that if they put the bargains up front, people won't venture any farther and will miss the pricier items with the bigger profit margins.

But Build-A-Bear Workshop stores are different. When a Guest walks through the door, they're greeted by one of our Bear Builder associates (whom we refer to as our First Impressions Bears). Those who can only afford a $10 bear are immediately attracted to these lower-priced items. However, we personally introduce Guests to our entire store, and they wind up walking by almost every piece of merchandise we stock. More often than not, Guests buy the bear they like the most, not the one that sells for the least amount of money. By putting the less expensive bears up front, it makes it clear from the start that we have something for every Guest's budget, without taking away from sales of the higher priced merchandise.

Like every sports team, Build-A-Bear Workshop has its own recognizable colors. The bright primary hues of yellow, red, and blue decorate everything we do—our logo, our stores, our gift cards, our web site, even our annual report.

Through the years, lots of people have told me those are "baby colors." I disagree. They're bright, happy colors, and they've become synonymous with our brand.

In 2004, we formed a partnership to begin selling some of our licensed products in Target department stores. While we were in the product development stage, some of the people I worked with at a toy manufacturer broached the subject of our brand colors.

"They're kind of baby colors," they told me. They were reciting one of those old rules in retailing: Primary colors are used in merchandising for infants and very young children, but not to attract an older target audience.

Trust your instincts above all else.

I respect the people who helped us create these products a lot, but I disagreed on this issue and wasn't about to change our primary colors. I explained to these executives that yellow, red, and blue are part of our brand and if they wanted to do business with Build-A-Bear Workshop, they'd have to live with them. They ultimately agreed. You know what? Those baby colors haven't negatively impacted our sales at Target one bit.

You'd be crazy to ignore conventional wisdom completely. I've gotten some of my best ideas from learning how the retail business works and by building on the old rules of doing business. But I always trust my own instincts above conventional wisdom, and am sure to put my own spin on even the most universally accepted ways of doing things. That's what will really help you to stand out in today's competitive business world.

Pour Your Heart Into It

I f you've been to a Build-A-Bear Workshop store, you know that a special part of the experience is choosing a heart and filling it with wishes for your furry friend.

The whole notion of having heart has become an apt emblem for our business because I really believe you have to pour your heart into whatever you do to make your company successful. That's why I felt it was so important to include this concept in the book's subtitle.

Let me first tell you how hearts came to be a part of the experience at Build-A-Bear Workshop.

In order to make your company successful, you've got to pour your heart into it.

In the summer of 1997, though I was pretty busy trying to get my new business off the ground, I took time to attend a Fourth of July picnic at a friend's home. Another friend who attended, Sarah Rus-

29

sell, who sadly died a few years ago, was an artist. I really respected her opinion. I brought along several bears that we planned to sell in our store, hoping to get her thoughts about them.

Sarah gushed over the cute, soft, cuddly creatures. In an amazing moment of insight she said, "You've got to put hearts in these bears. They just have so much personality."

For me, that was one of those lightbulb moments you see in cartoons. I knew exactly what Sarah meant. And I knew precisely what these hearts should look like because I'd just been shopping at a Saint Louis gift shop that was selling puffy, heart-shaped pins. I decided to ask one of our vendors to make similar stuffed fabric hearts for our Guests to put in their bears. We were just weeks away from opening our first store at the Saint Louis Galleria, so it was pretty late in the game. In fact, we'd already set the selling price for all of our animals, so adding the hearts increased our costs and cut into potential profits. But Sarah's idea was too brilliant to ignore.

> *Your employees, friends, and customers are often the sources of the most brilliant ideas for your business.*

A short time later, one of our associates had another stroke of genius. Jeff Marx was a teacher by day, but he'd come to work for us part-time as a Bear Builder associate. About three weeks after we opened, I showed up at the Galleria store to take care of some business. While I was there, I watched as Jeff interacted with our Guests. Instead of just offering them the option of adding a heart to their bears, as he'd been trained to do, Jeff created a ceremony around the whole process of selecting the right heart. He was truly engaging kids and adults in the process by having them pick their heart, kiss it, jump up and down, put the heart on their right and left elbows, and then make a wish.

Our Guests were really into it. I saw kids squinching their eyes and contemplating their wishes as they waited their turn to stuff their animals and wish upon their hearts. You could tell by their faces that it was really important to say the right wish and seal it with a kiss. Everyone wanted to do this.

I immediately knew that Jeff had come up with an amazing idea. I had him teach our other associates how to do this heart ceremony. It has now become an integral part of how we operate at Build-A-Bear Workshop. While virtually every bear has one signature heart, I once saw three siblings put three hearts into a Father's Day bear for their dad. I even stuffed an animal's chest with 100 hearts once for a young friend of mine with congenital heart disease. I figured she could use lots of extras!

> *Be prepared to bare your soul with others as it relates to your vision for the business.*

Your employees, friends, and customers are often the sources of the most brilliant ideas for your business. Both Sarah and Jeff had two great ideas that ultimately helped strengthen the Build-A-Bear Workshop brand. But they contributed more than just ideas. They really put their hearts into our company by doing what they felt was right. They were immediately engaged and involved with the brand.

That's how I try to approach business. I listen to my own vision and trust in my own instincts. Then I pour my heart into everything I do. I am truly emotionally involved in my job. I'm passionate about engaging with our Guests and providing them with happy, memorable experiences. That is the heart of this company and the work I do.

As I mentioned, though I'd been quite successful professionally, when I left corporate America to become an entrepreneur, I felt pretty emotionally bankrupt. I needed to return to the kind of work I could be fully invested in, something I could truly put my heart into.

> *If you convey your passion to others, they'll quickly come to understand what your company is all about.*

Build-A-Bear Workshop satisfied that longing more than I could have imagined. Much of my passion stems from the fact that I lost "Teddy," my own stuffed bear, back when I was 10 years old. I have been looking for Teddy ever since, though I now feel like I've found him a million times over though the happiness we've brought so many others through this company. To help ensure that no child ever feels this same loss, each time a Guest buys a bear, it is entered into our Find-A-Bear ID tracking system so these beloved animals can hopefully find their way home if they ever go out adventuring alone. This tracking system is a very important part of our brand that stems directly from my connection with and passion for Teddy.

When I began sharing my vision for this business with others, I had to bare my soul to people, in much the same way Sam Walton of Wal-Mart and Ray Kroc of McDonald's did when they were trying to win people over to their way of thinking about retailing and restaurants. I had to convey my passion and tell them the sad story of my lost teddy bear-so early investors and supporters could really understand my motivations and ideas for the company. Though I'd lost my special stuffed animal, I still remembered how important it was to me, and I wanted children everywhere to have the same opportunity to forge their own lifelong furry friendships.

I knew when I started Build-A-Bear Workshop that I wanted to bring the theater back to retailing. That was something I learned from Stanley Goodman, former chairman of the May Department Stores Company. During my third week on the job as an executive trainee, I heard Stanley give a speech. He talked about retailing as entertainment and the store as a stage. I vividly remember his statement, as if he were talking to me alone: "When a customer has fun, they spend more money." That was a defining moment for me and that concept has stayed with me ever since.

> *The best way to build a successful company is one passionate, emotionally attached person at a time.*

My goal when I started Build-A-Bear Workshop was, of course, to create a profitable business. But I really wanted more than that. My objective is to make people happy and put smiles on their faces. I want every single person who walks into our stores to feel like it was the best day of his or her life, whether they're 3 or 103. If I could wait on each Guest, I would. I want to know their stories and why they chose to spend money in our store. I also want to know whether they had fun and felt like they were treated well.

For so long, businesses (and businesspeople) were faulted for showing emotion. Doing so was considered unprofessional and inappropriate. I'm here to tell you it's essential to feel a connection to what you are doing and get your customers to feel that connection. Today, connecting with your customers—hitting that emotional "buy me" button—is considered to be such a huge idea, it is actually being written about as an algebraic equation. In researching her latest book, *Shops That Pop!: Preparing for the Future of Shopping*, nationally recognized consumer insights expert Pam Danziger discovered that "tangible factors play a role in the shopping decision, but they rarely dominate." Danziger, who is president of Unity Marketing, found that such tangibles as "need," "features," and "affordability" are *additive*: $1 + 1 + 1 = 3$. In contrast, "emotion" works *exponentially*: $(1 + 1 + 1)5^2 = 75$.

We see this every day at Build-A-Bear Workshop. When you can connect with your customers in an emotional way and ignite their passion, you will be on you way to building a successful company—one passionate, emotionally attached person at a time.

Envision the Core User

As you know by now, my young friend, Katie, was the inspiration for Build-A-Bear Workshop. Every day, we make new huggable companions for boys, girls, teenagers, moms, dads, grandmothers, and grandfathers. But we've opted to focus the majority of our energies and our dollars on one specific group of Guests—10-year-old girls, which is very fitting considering that Katie loved the idea so much at that age.

We want to do everything we can to create a place these girls would like to visit over and over again, thereby capturing their business, their parents' business, their brothers' and sisters' business, and their grandparents' business as well.

Think about the product or service you sell.
Who is buying it—or may want to?

Among other things, we paint the stores in attractive primary colors and size our fixtures just right for the under-four-feet crowd we often serve. We also make the aisles wide enough for strollers (given that many moms come with baby in tow), and see to it that all products are easily accessible to shoppers of all ages.

Think about the product or service you sell. Who is buying it—or may want to? As with Build-A-Bear Workshop, that list may be broad. If it is, that's wonderful. It means there's a huge potential market for your company. (Just be realistic when you make out this list. If you sell wedding dresses, for example, your market is limited to brides looking for a wedding dress, not "everyone.") But you can't market to your entire demographic audience, either. In order to be successful—and indeed to develop a brand identity—you must identify the core user of your product and tailor your marketing message, your product, and your delivery to reach that audience.

Which of your customers are likely to return to your business again and again? Which ones will be the most loyal? Who will tout your products to their friends and strangers?

The key is having a targeted focus. Be singular in your purpose. Put the blinders on, except in relation to your core customer group. Then, open your eyes wide to their demands and desires and do everything you can to satisfy them. In other words, specialize in making one core group enormously happy instead of trying to make a lot of different types of customers feel moderately satisfied.

To create brand identity, identify the core user of your product and tailor your marketing message, product, and delivery to that person alone.

In marketing, this is called the "less is more" approach. The tighter and more narrowly focused your business strategy, the more likely you are to connect to your customers with perfect precision.

Take a broader approach and you'll have more difficulty reaching any of them. In turn, you'll record fewer sales.

You won't be able to identify your core customer just by looking at market research. Such data may give you a general idea of who is buying or consuming your type of product—such as males 18–24, families with children, or women in their fifties. But the data won't really provide any insight into who these customers are. And the numbers won't address the motivation or personality of your core customer. You have to figure that out by talking and listening to *real* people, topics I address in detail in later chapters.

Here's an example of how relying on market research alone could cause you to overlook your core customer:

Ice cream is a hot product these days. The ice cream market in the United States grew 24 percent between 1998 and 2003, according to the trade publication *Prepared Foods*. While everybody loves ice cream, kids drive the industry, downing more scoops and Scooter Crunches than their parents.

How, then, can we explain the proliferation of brands aimed at adults—both gourmet superpremium ice cream flavors and low-fat, sugar-free varieties? Ice cream brands like Edy's and Ben & Jerry's are aiming not for the market in general, but for a specific niche—adults who love ice cream. From the vast population of ice cream eaters, these brands have identified their core consumer and they're tailoring products specifically to these more mature tastes.

Edy's sells 21 flavors of light slow-churned ice cream with half the fat and one-third the calories of regular ice cream. The company's core customer? Adults who are getting too thick around the middle to indulge in a bowl of regular ice cream every night.

The tighter and more narrowly focused your business strategy, the more likely you are to connect to your customers with perfect precision.

Ben & Jerry's, a company founded by two free spirits, offers funky flavors with even funkier names. Lots of people eat Ben & Jerry's ice cream, but the company's core customers are socially conscious ice cream lovers.

The core customer at our company is a 10-year-old girl who lives in the suburbs, goes to grade school, and enjoys playing with real, imaginary, and stuffed friends.

As I developed the business plan, I thought in terms of what Build-A-Bear Workshop could offer girls like Katie. I still do today. I also asked for Katie's own insights, and now that Katie is nearly 20, I continue to talk with other 10-year-old girls all the time. You simply can't get inside the mind of your core customer without spending time with him or her.

These are just some of the questions I've asked myself about our young female Guests: What does she like to do? What are her unmet needs? How does she play? How does she interact with others? What will cause her to come to the store the first time? What will make her return again and again? What would she want to do if she came to the store? Would she bring a friend? Would she bring her sisters and brothers?

Through this process, I learned a lot that I translated into ideas for the business.

When Katie was 10, play was really important to her and her friends. Thus, we don't rush our Guests through the store; we invite them to stay awhile and play.

Katie had a lot of 10-year-old friends, and they did a lot of things together as a group. That's one of the reasons we hold parties in all our stores.

Data is great, but it doesn't address the motivation or personality of your core customer.

Katie, like many children today, aspired to be older than she really was, though she was still a child at heart. That's why we sell brand-name furry fashions for our animals, the kind older kids like, but we make sure they are age appropriate.

Girls like Katie play make-believe and dress up. In turn, we sell bear-sized princess outfits, wedding dresses, and superhero costumes.

Katie loved her bear George. She pampered him and tucked him into bed with her every night. As a result, kids get to give their furry friends a fluff and brush their fur at the store—and they can even buy their own bear-sized beds and other accessories with which to pamper their prized possessions.

I imagine some of you consider this advice to be crazy. Why define and design your business around the preferences of a single customer? If that's what you think I mean, you're missing my point.

Consider how pollsters do their work. They interview a sampling of people and use the answers of the few to extrapolate how the population in general stands on a given issue. Even the U.S. Census Bureau uses this method to make projections about the population of the United States and the economic standing of its citizens.

Katie was an extraordinary little girl, but she was also very representative. From her opinions and preferences, we were able to extrapolate the opinions and preferences of thousands of other girls in her age group and create a company that has tremendous appeal for them.

Each week, we receive hundreds of e-mails from girls, as well as their parents and relatives. We circulate these and read them at company meetings. We want our Guests present as much as possible in our discussions.

By focusing more narrowly on one core user segment, we didn't limit the potential for the brand. We expanded it greatly. It might sound a little nuts, but it's not. And my company is the proof.

Every year, Build-A-Bear Workshop attracts millions of young girls like Katie to our stores. But they don't come alone, which is why we sell a lot to brothers, parents, parents-to-be, grandparents, aunts, and uncles, too.

Visualize your customer.

Sit down and figure out who the "Katie" is for your business. We keep pictures of our Guests hung up on the walls, so we're always surrounded by and reminded of them. When I worked at Payless ShoeSource, we used to cut pictures out of magazines depicting our typical shoppers, so these customers were always at the forefront of our thought process.

Can you visually identify (through pictures and otherwise) your core customers? It's really one of the most important things you'll ever do.

Imagine Your Company from the Inside Out

worked in a corporate setting a long time before founding Build-A-Bear Workshop. While I learned a lot in that buttoned-up world of rules and dress codes, I knew I didn't want my own business to function that way. It needed a different personality, one that reflected my own outlook on life and the warm and fuzzy brand we were trying to create.

> *Defining the personality of your company is one of the most important early decisions you can possibly make.*

Of all the decisions you have to make when starting a new business, you might not think it matters what your company looks and feels like. But I'm here to tell you that defining the personality of your company is one of the most important early decisions you can possibly make. Your company's personality, or culture, is like the foundation of a house. To take the analogy further and give it even more meaning, it's like your own personal morality. It is the foundation on which everything is built, the rule that guides every future decision and action. This choice about your company's personality will influence your brand and how customers experience your company.

When creating a business from scratch, you get to make it whatever you want it to be—from the color of the walls to the benefits package. At this stage, at least, you have infinite control over every aspect of the operations. You ought to let all of the good and bad experiences you've encountered in business guide you as you imagine your company from the inside out. It's all about building a better mousetrap.

> *Your company's personality, or culture, is like the foundation of a house.*

Did you hate the complicated expense forms you had to fill out at your last job? Create those easy-to-use ones you always longed for. Liked casual Fridays? Implement your own casual dress code for every day of the week. Felt guilty about calling in sick, even when you were? Don't make your own employees do it; give them a set amount of personal/sick days to use whenever and for whatever reason they desire.

As you can see from these examples, imagining your company from the inside out begins with determining how you want to live—and how you want your employees to live—during those 8, 10, 12, or even 16 hours every day they're at the office. I had a wealth of experience to draw from, so I had a pretty good vision of the atmosphere I wanted to create when I went into business for myself.

I knew I wanted the company to stand for fun and family, so I had to recreate that in our working environment. I wanted it to be all the things I liked—and nothing I didn't—both from my past jobs and from other companies I had long studied and admired.

When creating your business from scratch, let all of the good and bad experiences you've encountered over the years shape how you decide to do things.

I created a bright and fun place to work, which I'll talk about more shortly, and implemented flexible, family-friendly policies—things that would make our associates' lives easier. For example, associates get 15 Honey Days that they can use for whatever they choose, be it vacation, sick leave, a school play, or a much-needed shopping trip. While there are set working hours in our corporate office, or what we refer to as our World Bearquarters, associates are allowed to work a flexible schedule when needed. We trust them to get their work done on their own initiative. You don't even have to make an appearance at the office every day to prove you're working. Today, with computers and cell phones, you can work from almost anywhere.

We also created an environment that is as far from stuffy as you can imagine. As you can tell from my title—Chief Executive Bear—we don't take ourselves too seriously. We're serious about business, but that doesn't mean everything has to be buttoned down. The walls of our World Bearquarters are painted the same cheery yellow that you'll see in our stores. Inspirational teddy bear phrases—what we call the Bearisms that are found at the back of this book—also adorn the walls, reminding us how to conduct ourselves and interact with other people. Most of our associates work out of cubicles (they're so practical!), but they don't look like the cubes in the *Dilbert* comic strip. They are bright and colorful, not dull and gray. We encourage our associates to personalize their spaces by adding decorations, photos, and stuffed animals that reflect their personalities.

Our dress code is very casual; jeans are perfectly acceptable on most days. Though I spent decades dressed in suits and high heels, I'm not a very formal person. After I left Payless ShoeSource, I worked out of my home for about a year. I learned then what I think I'd always known: You can be just as productive in casual clothing (or even your pajamas) as in a business suit or a tie. I prefer working in a relaxed atmosphere, so that's what I created. I think people can work in a setting like ours and still be efficient, effective, and productive.

> *Consider allowing employees to work flexible schedules, and embrace a relaxed atmosphere.*

Though we've grown so much bigger over the past few years, I still think we have a small-company feel and that we function more like family than coworkers—both at the store level and in our corporate office. That was always my intention.

My husband, Bob, runs his own business from the office next door to mine, so we're like one big family. We hold company picnics together and schedule group outings involving our two companies. We're the "parents" of one big business family. Our associates sometimes call us Mama Bear and Papa Bear.

In imagining my company from the inside out, I knew I never wanted to lose sight of whom we're working for. At our stores, which are visited by thousands of kids every day, that's impossible to forget. But at our World Bearquarters, we have little day-to-day interaction with those who are experiencing the bear-making process. That's why I've found another way to keep them ever-present. In our lobby, we have a bulletin board—we call it our Wall of Fame—filled with photos of Guests and their letters of adoration.

> *Never lose sight of whom you are working for.*

My idol, Walt Disney, was not only an entertainment genius, he was also a historian. He saved a tremendous amount of material from his company's early days, building a huge archive of Disney history. I've followed his example and saved these letters and photos—the most important keepsakes of our business. They hang in our lobby as a way of telling our history. The bulletin board also serves as a constant reminder of whom we work for and where we come from. These are the people who helped turn Build-A-Bear Workshop into a $350 million-plus company.

I must reiterate how important planning and self-reflection are in creating a business. When you start writing a business plan, you are blessed with a blank slate and ought to do everything you can to fill that void exactly the way you want to. Put your imagination to work to create the ultimate workplace and culture for yourself and your employees. It's up to you!

It's All in the Details

Picture a soldier in his dress uniform. His posture is straight. His trousers are perfectly pressed, with creases as sharp as knife blades ironed in. His medals and insignia are lined up like troops in formation, and his shoes gleam from a recent polishing. All these little details combine to form an impressive appearance.

> *Details can make the difference between a good versus a bad impression, and even success versus failure.*

Details can make the difference between a good versus a bad impression, and even success versus failure. I'm not a perfectionist, but I am a stickler for details because I know how important the so-called little things are to consumers. They are beary big to us. The details are where you can stand out or fail, where you can impress or disappoint a potential customer. Though I'm an advocate of big-picture thinking when planning a business, I also believe that tending to the small things and paying attention to details that others may overlook will help you to soar above the competition. They will help to strengthen your brand and raise your stock among consumers, who will come to identify your business as one that covers all its bases.

FedEx is one company focused on the seemingly small details of its business. A while back, some branding consultants hired by the company concluded that they didn't like the sound customers heard when dropping a package into one of FedEx's drop boxes. They worried that customers would associate that hollow echo with cheapness, and therefore might have doubts about the safety and security of their packages inside the metal box. In response, FedEx fortified these boxes with an extra millimeter of steel and added a rubber stopper to prevent any clattering when the lid slammed shut. That way, for all you knew, the box was full and very secure. It's the small details like this that make a big difference in the highly competitive overnight shipping industry.

> *Tending to the little (big) things that others may overlook will help you to soar above the competition.*

We're just as focused on details at Build-A-Bear Workshop because they matter to our Guests. It would probably take a dozen visits to our stores for you to take in all the little details we have put into place. Our miniaturized binoculars, for example, look and work like the real thing. There are treads on the bottom of every pair of bear sneakers. We have "bearized" the lyrics to all the songs played in our stores. The dolls in our "friends 2B made" locations—a new concept we are starting to roll out, in many cases next to or within existing Build-A-Bear Workshop locations—have painted toenails. We have put teddy bear wallpaper up in our bathrooms. And the buttons, pockets, and zippers on our bear clothes are fully functional.

Authenticity is a very important emblem of our brand, hence our decision to focus on the details necessary to make our animals and other products seem as real as possible. I encourage you to identify the emblems of your brand and be careful to tend to all of the details that support them. That's what all of the most successful detail-oriented companies do.

> *Don't get bogged down with all the little stuff that doesn't matter.*

Just don't get bogged down in all the little stuff that doesn't matter. I've heard stories about fast-food restaurants that castigate their servers for giving diners more than one napkin or two packets of ketchup. I appreciate that companies must be fiscally responsible, but practices like these border on stinginess. They exemplify how easy it is to get bogged down in details—saving money on supplies and ingredients while losing sight of the ultimate mission of serving your customers and treating them well. I don't believe in nickel-and-diming Guests by charging them for every little thing or keeping a strict inventory of each item we give away. And I don't believe in handcuffing employees with silly rules, like making them count ketchup packets. Our associates aren't required to keep track of how many free stickers or hair bows they hand out. If they were, none of us would ever have time to wait on a Guest. Instead, we pay attention to the little (big) things that do matter.

I travel a lot, and one of my favorite places to have dinner while on the road is Cracker Barrel Old Country Store. The company operates a chain of roadside restaurants that serve wholesome Southern food, just like Grandma used to make—assuming your grandma was the type who prepared buttermilk biscuits from scratch, fried steak, and collards. I like the food at Cracker Barrel, but what really stands out for me are the chain's bathrooms. They're always clean and have soft towels, great-smelling soap, and lavender-scented lotion that you can buy in the gift shop while waiting for your table. Cracker Barrel really focuses on those details that make a difference to its core clientele, namely travelers. The clean and comfortable bathrooms are just one example. The restaurant also gives away free highway maps, with other Cracker Barrel locations plotted along the route. Customers can check out audiobooks at one Cracker Barrel restaurant and return them at another hours down the highway.

> *Never handcuff employees with silly rules.*

Cracker Barrel offers more than just a meal; by paying attention to the details that matter to road-weary drivers, the company makes traveling easier. Dining anywhere else during a road trip would be like ordering hot apple cobbler without the ice cream. You wouldn't want to do it.

QuikTrip convenience stores are another traveler favorite. Many convenience stores aren't very pleasant places to visit. But QuikTrip stores are brightly lit. The coffee is always good and fresh; it doesn't taste like sludge that's been left in the pot too long. The doughnuts aren't stale, and the hot dogs smell like they're from a baseball game—not a convenience store. These are small details, but big enough to make me choose QuikTrip over the competition.

That's the true lesson of this chapter. In a side-by-side comparison with your competition, it's often the small stuff that will really make a big difference. Success is in the details! We've certainly elevated details to big-deal status at Build-A-Bear Workshop. For instance, in our Fifth Avenue store in New York, we opened the Eat with Your Bear Hands Café, where we serve only finger foods like hot dogs, hamburgers, pizza, grilled cheese sandwiches, and cookies. That way, as the name implies, Guests can eat everything with their bare (or, as I prefer it, bear) hands.

Success is in the details!

The food at the Eat with Your Bear Hands Café is good, but simple, which is why I wanted every other thing about the restaurant to be special. We created adorable bear-head straws and napkins that urge users to "Wipe Your Paws." Guests receive plastic bibs for themselves *and* their bears. The place mats have etiquette lessons, written in "bearese": "Fork Over Your Spoon." "Paws Between Bites." "Tame That Growling Tummy." "Save Room Fur Dessert." Our colorful drink cups carry the restaurant's logo and the messages, "Paws Between Slurps" and "Paws Between Sips." Take-out orders go out in colorful miniature shopping bags, instead of the ubiquitous white or brown variety you see all over the city.

The ketchup, mustard, and Bear-B-Q sauce bottles have the instruction "Squeeze Me," and are corralled in a neat bear-shaped holder. We even have miniature chairs where the stuffed bears can sit while their human best friends have lunch. Of course, they have their own bear-sized plates, too. Minding all these details is fun for us, and enjoying them is fun for our Guests.

Develop Strong Partnerships

Most successful companies wouldn't be where they are today without the help of trusted partners. Partnerships can take many forms: A partner may be a vendor, a contractor, a landlord, another company with which you've combined promotional efforts, a business whose name or product you're licensing (or vice versa), or a charity you're supporting.

To work, good business partnerships require compatibility, trust, and cooperation.

Good business partnerships are like successful marriages. To work, they require compatibility, trust, and cooperation. Both parties need to be invested in one another's well-being and strive for a common goal. They must look out for one another and be mutually supportive during the tough times. Sadly, like bad marriages, poor business relationships often fail, costing both sides time and money.

On the flip side, however, there are those that thrive and deliver huge financial returns. The most successful corporate partnerships are forged between like-minded companies with similar cultures that have joined together for a common goal, where both sides benefit from the relationship. Think of McDonald's and Disney, or even Build-A-Bear Workshop and Limited Too.

When creating your own partnerships, remember this equation: Both sides ought to win and be better off because of the alliance. Your relationships with your vendors, suppliers, contractors, landlords, and other partners should be collaborative and cooperative, not adversarial. You ought to be working together because you can make more money as a team than you could apart or by working with someone else.

> *The most successful corporate partnerships are forged between like-minded companies joined together for a mutually beneficial common goal.*

I tend to think of partners as good business friends—companies and people who would do everything they could to help us succeed and for whom I would do the same. For the most part, that's precisely the experience I've had during my decades dealing with partnerships in the retail business. Luck may have played some role, but I think I've had good experiences because I've always chosen my partners carefully. In turn, I've created my own good luck. (Look for more on that concept in a future chapter.)

> *Good partners are like good friends; they'll do everything they can to help the other succeed.*

Most of our products are made in overseas factories in such places as China, South Korea, and Taiwan. I worked with most of these vendors in my previous jobs, and chose them as partners based on my past experiences, the quality of their work, price, and, perhaps most importantly, their trustworthiness. I obviously can't be overseas managing and monitoring the manufacturing process all the time, so I have to count on our vendors to do it for me. I've put a tremendous amount of faith in these partners. If you don't trust a company or its employees, you shouldn't do business with them. If I think someone is not being honest, or that they might try to deceive us, that's a deal breaker.

While I prefer only the necessary contracts (and certainly as few pages as possible), once you find a good partner you can trust, written up-front agreements are often a clean way to be sure all discussed terms are acceptable to both parties. It's also a good idea after a meeting to be sure someone records the facts and agreed-to points, and distributes them to all participants in writing. E-mail is a good method for doing this. Steps like this will make your life easier. After all, the bigger your business gets, the harder it is to remember all details about every vendor, contract, and meeting. Written records give you good notes for doing follow-ups, too.

> *If you don't trust a company or its employees, don't do business with them.*

If you don't have a lot of prior experience working with a particular supplier, I think it's a good idea to try out several vendors before making a long-term commitment with any single one. That way, you're able to compare quality, responsiveness, and the more intangible characteristics—like trustworthiness and business ethics. You need to place as much importance on finding and forging these business relationships as you do on hiring employees.

Vetting potential partners, in many ways, mirrors the job-interviewing process.

> *Put your business terms in writing so everyone is clear.*

One word of caution: Every company must be careful about relying too heavily on any single partner or vendor for products or services. Imagine what would happen if your company's sole supplier suffered a manufacturing interruption or went out of business. To prevent such calamities, you'll want to buy from multiple suppliers. At the very least, have a ready stable of backup suppliers should problems arise. On the flip side, it's unwise to spread your business among *too* many vendors. That weakens your partnerships, making you less important to the companies you buy from.

We are a significant source of revenue for most of our vendors. They want our business, and hopefully we are meaningful to their success. This makes them much more responsive when we call and say we need more bear ponchos—pronto—or that our warehouse roof has collapsed (as it did in 1997) and we need more of every item in our inventory sent quicker than they can manufacture it.

While we're loyal to our existing vendors—who have earned our loyalty—we're also smart about business. We're constantly evaluating other companies that might be able to offer us better products and technologies that will lead to increased efficiencies. Our vendors know this, and I think it keeps them on their toes, constantly evolving their processes to improve their own business—and to keep ours. As part of your original deal, be up front in the contract about how often you'll review the vendor's performance. Your partners need to know that once they win your business, the work isn't over. Business partnerships are like marriages: To work well, they require give-and-take and constant communication.

Don't rely too heavily on any single partner or vendor.

I can't stress enough how important good partnerships will be to your company's success. My mother always told me to choose my friends carefully, and that lesson applies here. The company you keep will affect your business reputation. If you align yourself with good partners—where the give-and-take of the relationship is balanced—you're much more likely to enjoy success than failure. It's what I refer to as my 1 + 1 = 10 formula, which I'll talk more about in Part Six.

Be Financially Secure

Unless you were born with a trust fund, there has probably been a time in your life when you've had financial problems. Maybe you spent your last dollar on Tuesday, but payday is not until Friday. Perhaps the rent and your car payment are both due the same day, but you've only got enough in your account to cover one or the other. It could be that your credit cards are maxed out, or that you overspent on holiday gifts.

Having your financial books in order will help to attract quality investors, employees, vendors, and business partners.

Whatever the case, chances are I've been there, too. Though I've always been careful with money, there were times early in my career when my spending outpaced my income. I remember standing in my room and tossing all my bills into the air. I told myself that only those landing on the bed would get paid that day. (Sound familiar?)

This is not a situation you want to find yourself in in your personal life, and you must certainly avoid it in business as well. Financial security is crucial whether you're just starting out or leading a mature company. Having your financial books in order will affect the growth of your business, along with your ability to attract quality investors, recruit and retain employees, and solidify relationships with vendors and business partners. It will also give you the capacity to respond to customer demands and the changing marketplace.

> *Going into business underfunded is the biggest and most damaging mistake entrepreneurs make.*

Going into business underfunded (or without a good financial plan) is the biggest and most damaging mistake entrepreneurs make. They get so caught up in making ends meet and covering basic expenses, they miss opportunities to wow their customers because they are unable to take any financial risks or spend a penny more than is necessary to simply get by. If you don't have enough money, your business *will* struggle. And the chances are greater that it will fail.

Undercapitalized companies can't respond adequately to customer demands or complaints, or even implement suggestions that would improve the business. They can't afford to spend money, even if doing so will make even more. A low bank account balance will hamstring growth, leaving your company with little room for mistakes—or new opportunities. I know of many small businesses that walk a financial tightrope each month. Their cash flow is so limited, if one payment for goods or services doesn't arrive on the exact day it's expected, the company can't make payroll or cover its own bills. Each month, this vicious cycle is perpetuated.

Admittedly, I had a bigger nest egg than most aspiring entrepreneurs when I started Build-A-Bear Workshop thanks to my previous career as a retail executive. But you can be financially secure without having that same level of personal wealth. The key is planning ahead.

> *If you don't have enough money, your business will struggle.*

As you develop your business plan, you'll be creating a picture of what your company will look like at each phase of growth. As such, you should be able to estimate how much money you'll require at every stage and how you'll get that money when you need it.

It's like socking away cash for retirement. Most people would like to quit working by the time they're 65 or so. Without a paycheck, you need other means to cover everyday expenses, unexpected costs (like a hospital stay), and unexpected opportunities (like a cruise to Alaska). People use a myriad of methods to ensure financial security in retirement—pension plans, 401(k)s, insurance, government assistance, investments, reverse mortgages, even part-time jobs. Businesses have their own ways of ensuring long-term financial security—increased revenues, outside investors, spin-offs, reduced expenses, and price increases, just to name a few.

Start-ups are often plagued by cash-flow problems. Perhaps you've got a great idea, but it will be a while before you start bringing in revenue. The bank account balance is heading in only one direction—down. Credit cards are the answer for a good many new companies. About half of small businesses are financed with plastic, according to a survey by the National Small Business Association, while just 6 percent use U.S. Small Business Administration (SBA) loans, and 2 percent receive venture capital.

I'm not a big fan of using credit cards to start a business, and am grateful I didn't need to do so when starting Build-A-Bear Workshop. (I used a portion of my retirement savings instead.) If credit cards are your only choice to fund your new venture, beware. Seek out the absolute best interest rates you can find, and don't charge any more amounts than you'll be able to pay off in a reasonable time period. (You'll need to decide how to define "reasonable." A month? A year? Five years?) It's a good idea to get a separate credit card for business expenses. Interest on business expenses is tax deductible, and having separate cards will simplify things at tax time. Plus, it's always best to keep your business liabilities separate from your personal liabilities. You wouldn't want your business credit rating to affect your personal credit rating, or vice versa. The Internal Revenue Service also prefers it this way.

> *Undercapitalized companies can't respond adequately to customer demands, complaints, or suggestions.*

Lots of people risk their personal financial stability to follow their business dreams. I'm all for following your dreams, but please be careful about what you put at stake. If you're planning to gamble the kids' college fund or use your family home as collateral for a loan, evaluate the business opportunity with your head, not your heart. Just like an outside investor, require more proof than a gut feeling that this is a viable venture that will deliver a return. Think smartly, not emotionally.

Outsiders can help to improve your company's financial stability. And they don't always have to write a check to do so. Attorneys often work on a contingency basis—they get paid when their clients get paid—and many suppliers are willing to work this way as well. Legend has it that once he'd bought all the necessary equipment and leased a storefront, Vernon Rudolph, the founder of Krispy Kreme Doughnuts, didn't have enough cash left for ingredients. He struck a deal with a sympathetic grocer (and might I say, a pretty savvy investor). The businessman agreed to give Rudolph the eggs, flour, and other groceries he'd need for his doughnuts, and Rudolph promised to pay him back from the first day's profits. As it turned out, Rudolph wound up making enough to cover the loan—and then some.

> *A low bank account balance will hamstring growth, leaving your company with little room for mistakes—or new opportunities.*

You can use similar negotiating tactics with building owners. Our landlords invested in helping us build our stores, in a sense, by offering us variable lease agreements based on what we could pay at each stage of growth. We paid less at the beginning, and more as our stores started making more money. This helped tremendously with cash flow. Our cash wasn't tied up in high rents but was available to us as needed.

Should you get into financial straits, own up to it. Negotiate with your vendors and pay a little bit every month. Don't let your bills languish and compound with interest and late fees.

If you get behind on your bills, you could wind up losing business—and in legal trouble. Unfortunately, we've occasionally had suppliers that were going through financial difficulties. They weren't able to fulfill our orders because they were in arrears with their own suppliers. So we had to take our business elsewhere, probably further compounding that vendor's financial problems.

Here's my last bit of wisdom about money—and you're probably not going to like it: No matter how much planning you do, no matter how sophisticated your financial forecasting, you're going to need more money than you think. If you're fortunate enough to generate greater sales than projected, it will take additional money to hire more staff and handle the influx of business. Miss the mark the other way, and you'll need more money to improve marketing and pay rising expenses.

> *If credit cards are your only choice to fund your new venture, beware.*

In addition, everything you need to set up a business—telephone, Internet service, computer software, insurance, office space, and so forth—costs more than you would pay to buy it for your own personal use. That's the hard reality of "doing business as," instead of just being Maxine Clark.

Be smart, and be prepared. Go into business with more rather than less—and you'll make more in the process.

Put Your Plans in Writing

When I decided to write this book, I didn't simply turn on my computer and start writing from page 1. First, I needed to plan out my thoughts and develop a rough outline for the book, complete with a list of specific chapters and the topics I wanted to cover. This gave me a road map to follow, and made the whole writing process go that much more smoothly.

Likewise, when it comes to launching a new venture, having a well-thought-out written business plan is an essential first step. I spent almost a year researching, writing, and refining the business plan for Build-A-Bear Workshop. In fact, every business is always a work in progress.

Having a well-thought-out business plan is an essential component to launching your new venture.

I know how it is. You come up with a good idea or see something you want to pursue, get overwhelmed by excitement, and are anxious to go into business immediately. Believe me: In this case, patience is a real virtue. It's imperative for you to take the time to first write a carefully thought-out, clear, and accurate business plan. The discipline of doing so will force you to do your homework about the competitive environment in your industry. Your business plan will reveal what you need to do year by year to turn your idea into a viable and growing company.

Additionally, others are going to want to see your business plan. Investors, bankers, and perhaps even landlords and suppliers will want to read your plan to determine whether you truly have an understanding of your industry and the wherewithal to see the business through.

I understand how daunting this task must seem if you've never written a business plan before. It was a challenge for me, even though I had experience writing similar proposals and plans in my executive positions with other companies. I won't attempt to walk you through the process of writing your plan here, since that would take far too much space. Instead, let me recommend a number of books on the subject—many of which I consulted myself when writing the business plan for Build-A-Bear Workshop. All of these titles do a particularly good job of explaining both the basics and specifics of business plan writing. Here they are, in no particular order:

> *Venture Capital Handbook: New and Revised* by David Gladstone. (Financial Times Prentice Hall, 1987). (This is the one I primarily used.)
>
> *The Complete Book of Business Plans: Simple Steps to Writing a Powerful Business Plan* by Joseph A. Covello and Brian J. Hazelgren (Sourcebooks, 1994).
>
> *The McGraw-Hill Guide to Writing a High-Impact Business Plan: A Proven Blueprint for First-Time Entrepreneurs* by James B. Arkebauer (McGraw-Hill, 1994).
>
> *The Ernst & Young Business Plan Guide* by Eric S. Siegel, Brian R. Ford, and Jay M. Bornstein (John Wiley & Sons, 1993).

Writing a Convincing Business Plan by Art DeThomas and Lin Grensing-Pophal (Barron's Educational Series, 2001).

The Old Girls Network: Insider Advice for Women Building Businesses in a Man's World by Sharon Whiteley, Kathy Elliott, and Connie Duckworth (Perseus Books, 2003).

> *Your business plan will reveal what you need to do year-by-year to turn your idea into a viable and growing company.*

Your business plan is the financial, organizational, and operational blueprint for your company. I like to think of mine as the story of Build-A-Bear Workshop, written before the company ever existed. The document is still amazingly prophetic.

Of course, it's no coincidence that the company continues to match my eight-year-old conception of it. A business plan maps the future growth of your company, a thousand tiny steps and milestones at a time. It insulates you from surprises because you've already thought through them in advance.

My original business plan included a detailed assessment of the $2.5 billion plush animal retail market and the niche we could fill. It included a list of every location where we wanted to build a store along with a time line for achieving that growth. It outlined precisely how we would raise and spend money. It discussed our annual hiring plans and how we would improve our revenues through store growth and product innovation. It also projected specific revenues and profit for each year.

> *Think of your business plan as the operational blueprint for your company.*

Any business plan should include several essential elements. Again, the recommended books offer specific instructions for researching and writing each of these components:

- An energetic summary of your business idea and the niche it fills.
- A look at the company's ownership structure (i.e., sole proprietorship, corporation, partnership, or limited liability company).
- An accounting of capital needs.
- Specific details on how that capital will be utilized.
- A review of trends in your industry.
- An assessment of the competitive environment.
- Financial projections.
- Hiring projections.

> *A good plan forces you to confront and address the opportunities and challenges facing your business.*

For entrepreneurs, having a solid business plan is as essential as having a good idea to start with. A good plan forces you to confront and address the challenges and opportunities facing your business. It makes it possible for investors to understand your vision. And it shapes the thinking of management and employees, allowing everyone to have a shared road map for success.

Make Investors
Come to You

Depending on how big—and viable—your business idea is, you may be able to attract the interest of venture capitalists (VCs) who are willing to help you fund your business in exchange for a stake in it.

Admittedly, the competition has gotten tougher in the eight years since I founded Build-A-Bear Workshop. Our company came of age during the Internet boom, when VCs were dealing out money like cards at a poker game. That year, they invested $14.6 billion in companies at various stages of growth, according to statistics from PricewaterhouseCoopers. Not surprisingly, much of that went into technology-related areas.

You might be able to attract the attention of outside investors willing to help fund your business.

The truth is, getting venture capitalists to dip into their deep pockets for an upstart business is never easy. In fact, the odds are very much against you. It's more likely that one or more smaller angel investors will take you under their wings, although that can be challenging as well. But to have any chance at all, you must do your homework and be willing to put your own money on the line as well.

In 1997, I withdrew $750,000 from my retirement account to get Build-A-Bear Workshop off the ground. I also secured a bank line of credit, using my house as collateral. Even back then, I knew I wanted to build a multimillion-dollar business with hundreds of units, and I realized I didn't have the ready cash to fund that growth. It was clear that to achieve this goal, I'd have to partner with outside investors.

Unlike many entrepreneurs, however, I didn't have to seek out these investors. They came to me.

Serendipity played a role, though I also like to believe I did the right kind of legwork in the beginning to spread the word about Build-A-Bear Workshop and position the company as an attractive investment opportunity for venture capitalists.

You could do the same. You just have to follow a lesson my mother taught me early on: Do your own homework.

What homework is required when you're on the hunt for investors?

> *The first step to getting money is to write a solid business plan.*

The first step to getting money is to write a solid business plan. No bank or financial person is going to talk to you unless you have one. (See the previous chapter for my specific advice on how to spin your idea into a business plan.)

The second step is to show that plan around and investigate your funding options, even if you think you don't need outside money.

In my entrepreneurial quest, I talked to lots of different bankers and venture capitalists to find out what kind of money was available, what covenants were attached to that money, and how I could get my share of it.

Follow my lead: When working on your business plan, don't be afraid to share your ideas with people who might be able to help— now or in the future. Lots of entrepreneurs guard their ideas and business plans like the Hope diamond, for fear that if they talk about them too much, someone might steal them. It's much more likely that in the course of networking you'll meet people with worthy suggestions who can help you build the business.

As the vision for Build-A-Bear Workshop percolated in my brain, I prevailed upon my friends and business contacts for help. Specifically, I shared the plan with fellow members of the Committee of 200, a group of female corporate executives in the top echelon of business.

Disclosing my dream to this group served two purposes. First, I received valuable advice and feedback from some very smart women. Second, I landed on the radar screens of some of the most powerful people in American business who knew other high-level executives, including venture capitalists.

An old bromide in business is that you've got to network. Though it sounds like a cliché, you shouldn't discount the impact that networking can have. Networking is one of the ways I attracted investors to my business.

> *Don't be afraid to share your ideas with others in a position to help you.*

Nina McLemore, a friend of mine from the May Department Stores Company, later went on to found Liz Claiborne Accessories and run Regent Capital Management, a private equity firm in Manhattan. Though ours wasn't the kind of business her company funded, I still talked to Nina about Build-A-Bear Workshop. She gave me a list of firms that invested in early-stage companies. I met with or contacted every single one in 1997, though at the time I didn't really need their money and knew that most had their sights set only on Internet start-ups and other high-tech businesses. Still, these meetings were an effective way of networking and spreading the word about my new retail entertainment concept. The meetings paid off later when I *did* need money.

One of the people I talked with during that time was Frank Vest of Catterton Partners. Frank told me that his fund, which focused on the consumer industry, invested in later-stage companies than ours. But he was definitely interested in our business. I stayed in touch with Frank, frequently sending him articles that were written about Build-A-Bear Workshop. The relationship bore fruit in April 2000 when Catterton Partners made its first investment in our company.

In the summer of 1997, I got pretty lucky. A reporter with the *St. Louis Business Journal* saw the "Coming Soon" signs at the local mall and came to interview me about Build-A-Bear Workshop. When she first called, I suspected she was more interested in finding out why I'd left my previous job as president of Payless ShoeSource than about this new business. But I consented anyway.

> *Networking is the best way to attract investors to your business.*

Once the reporter learned about my concept, she abandoned her original angle and started asking me some really great questions about Build-A-Bear Workshop. In the end, she ran a very nice, well-reported, and well-researched article, which mentioned that eventually I would be seeking outside investors.

That one line in the article paid off, to the tune of millions of dollars. The same day the article ran, I received a call from Barney

Ebsworth, a Saint Louis businessman and the founder of Intrav Travel Company and Windsor Capital, his private investment firm. The next week Barney, his chief financial officer, Wayne Smith, and I met. I shared my vision with them. Barney asked how much money I thought I would need at that time. I showed him by business plan and said, "Four to five million dollars." To my surprise, and a little kiddingly, he replied, "Is next Thursday okay?" It turned out he shared my enthusiasm and confidence in the concept, and wanted to be a part of it. These are the people you want with you from the beginning. By September 30, 1997, about 45 days later, Barney and his partner, Wayne Smith, had committed $4.2 million in start-up money for a relatively small stake (20 percent) in the company. That investment raised the valuation of Build-A-Bear Workshop considerably and set the company up for growth through the following year. You could say that Barney is like my own local "Warren Buffett."

I had an eerily similar experience in 1998 when a newspaper in Kansas City wrote that we were opening our second store there. That article caught the attention of Kansas City Equity Partners, which became another of our early investors.

I encourage you to seek out media coverage in the business press early on. Potential investors read the business sections of their local newspapers. They also scour specialty business newspapers and magazines. American City Business Journals, which publishes the *St. Louis Business Journal*, has newspapers in dozens of cities. The company's bread and butter is profiling entrepreneurs and start-up businesses. If you're not lucky enough to have a reporter from one of these publications call you, pick up the phone yourself. You never know who might read the newspaper article and call you with an offer of millions.

> *Seek out media coverage in the business press early in your company's history so potential investors can learn about you.*

After our first Build-A-Bear Workshop store opened at Saint Louis Galleria, it began attracting the interest of other would-be investors. Our opening happened to coincide with parents' weekend at Washington University. Several parents who were New York investment bankers visited the store while in Saint Louis to see what all the hullabaloo was about and to talk with me about the concept. At the time, we were pretty flush with cash and didn't need additional investors. But I talked to all those would-be investors and kept the lines of communication open.

Tom Holley, a local businessman, introduced us to The Walnut Group, a venture capital firm from Cincinnati, Ohio. The firm took a significant $5 million stake in Build-A-Bear Workshop in 1998 and invested additional funds in 1999 and 2001.

In addition to private-equity firms, many of my friends also expressed interest in investing in the company. Their confidence meant a great deal to me, and I was honored that they wanted to stake their hard-earned money on my dream.

It is perfectly all right to accept investments from friends and family. If you do, however, structure the investments in such a way as to preserve the relationship and protect your friends and family from undue financial risk.

> *Entrepreneurs able to fund at least part of their business growth with their own money—or with the help of family and friends—are in a very powerful position.*

I didn't want the people I cared about to lose money if my business wasn't successful. So, my husband and I created three funds through which our friends and relatives could invest. They put money into these limited liability corporations and, in turn, we invested that money in Build-A-Bear Workshop. But we waited three years, until 2000, before accepting such investments in order to lessen the inherent risk of investing in a start-up. We also added our own money to each of these funds, to share in this risk.

I was fortunate enough to have my own money to invest as seed capital in Build-A-Bear Workshop. While I know this doesn't apply to most, if you do have the cash—or can get access to it—I highly recommend investing in your own idea. After all, how can you expect someone else to put money into your company if you're not willing to do the same? You need to get your skin in the game, so to speak.

Entrepreneurs able to fund at least part of their business growth with their own money—or with investments from friends and family—find themselves in a very powerful position. They can be choosier about the partners they take on and search for the best venture alliances.

In the case of Build-A-Bear Workshop, I knew that the earlier I took money from outside investors, the less control I would have. I didn't want that. Instead, I sought the freedom to fulfill my supreme dream. So many entrepreneurs take on the wrong partners because they're desperate for cash. Don't let that happen to you!

Part Two

Being a Great Boss

Show a Willingness to Do Any Job

Around the office or in one of our stores, you'll never hear me say, "That's not my job." There's nothing I wouldn't do to help my associates or Guests, no matter how small or large the task.

> *The best mentors are willing to roll up their sleeves and help with the task at hand.*

I've always had that mind-set, whether I was running the company, working in middle management, or just starting out. Back when I was climbing the corporate ladder, I found that my supervisors appreciated my willingness to pitch in without complaining wherever I was needed to complete any task. It signaled to them that I had initiative, and that I was a hard worker and team player who could be counted on in a crunch. In fact, that attitude probably played a huge role in my success. I probably wouldn't have been promoted so many times had I not shown by my actions that I'm a do-whatever-is-necessary worker.

The best mentors I ever had were those who would roll up their sleeves and help with the task at hand. It started in school with my Girl Scout leader, who went door-to-door with us helping to sell cookies. It continued with several executives at May, who would always stop to help a customer whenever they were on the sales floor. What I respected about each of them as leaders was that they didn't let things like titles or salaries get in the way of the work at hand. They pitched in to get the job done and, in turn, set an example for all of us to follow.

> *Great leaders are always there, guiding their employees through the process, and lighting the pathway toward success.*

On specific tasks, these great leaders wouldn't necessarily do the work for me, but they'd be right there beside me, guiding me through the process and coaching me to success. They'd help me work through problems and correct mistakes before they derailed the entire project. That's the role I try to fill now that I'm a Chief Executive Bear. I like to be an involved partner in the accomplishments and successes of my associates.

> *Get involved in the successes and accomplishments of those who work for you.*

My title has changed, but my attitude hasn't. I'm still willing to fill any role at the company. My associates have seen me in the trenches waiting on Guests, unpacking boxes, stocking shelves, running the Stuff Me machine, and ringing up sales on the cash register.

The more you do, the more you learn about the way your employees and customers do things, too.

> *You can't expect someone else to do a job well unless you're willing to do it yourself.*

I don't think you can ask someone else to do a job and expect them to do it well unless you're willing to do it yourself. This includes those dirty jobs that no one wants, like cleaning the toilets or taking out the garbage. The reality of starting a business is you will probably have to do every job at some point because you won't have the luxury of hiring staff to do it all. Even after your company has grown and you have people working for you, it's still important to get your hands dirty every once in a while. Leaders abdicate authority when they abdicate involvement.

Good leaders set the example that no job is beneath them, and no job is too small or menial. If your employees see you participating in the same tasks that they have to do, they'll get the message they are important to the company—and so is what they do. It will probably encourage them to do the job better themselves and to have an enhanced level of pride in the contribution they're making to the company.

> *Good leaders set the example that no job is beneath them.*

I use my frequent store visits as teaching opportunities. I truly love interacting with our Guests, and that's why I try to go to at least one of our locations every week. While I'm there, I'm also able to model proper Guest relations to our associates. I hope that when they see me chatting, helping, and playing with Guests, they'll note and incorporate some of my habits and strategies into their work ethic. At the same time, I learn so much from them and am able to spread the company's best practices even faster.

> *When you work alongside your employees, they'll see that you're human, just like them.*

From the time we're kids, we learn by observing, as well as by doing. It's important to set a good example for your employees and to do it frequently. When you work alongside your employees, they also get to see that you're human, just like them. It makes you more approachable, too.

> *When you work at every job, you'll quickly see which processes do and don't work.*

By stepping out of the executive office and back into work on occasion, you can learn a lot as well. We make many decisions at our World Bearquarters that affect how our associates do their jobs. While we all have the common commitment to serve our Guests and sell smiles, sometimes we unintentionally issue orders that are hard to follow or adopt policies that really gum things up. Just as I am the Chief Executive Bear (CEB), our store managers are called Chief Workshop Managers. They are the CEBs of their stores. Our associates feel empowered because of their commitment to tell us when we're doing something wrong—even those who don't normally feel comfortable speaking up to authority. When you work at every job, you learn very quickly which processes do and don't work. You also get a bird's-eye view of the additional resources your team needs to do their jobs effectively and efficiently. Plus, as the leader of the company, you have power that a normal employee doesn't. You can fix problems, thus making everyone's job easier.

Seek and Find Those
Who Share Your Passion

I have many good friends. If you gathered them all in one room, I'm sure they'd look like a mismatched bunch. Young and old. Men and women. Children and adults. Sophisticated and simple. Tall and short. Well educated and street smart. Democrats and Republicans.

Look to hire those who share common values, interests, experiences, and passions.

But where it matters—on the inside—they're very much alike. And that's where I connect with them. They are my friends because we share common values, interests, experiences, and passions. They care about and believe in the same things that I do. And, like me, they have heart.

My friendships have shown me how important it is to look inside to find out what people really stand for. That's crucial when you're choosing people to welcome into your life. It's essential when select-ing employees for your company as well. You should absolutely consider a candidate's resume, experience, and qualifications when hiring. But don't neglect the assessment of how well that candidate will fit into the culture you're trying to create. The people who work for your business both reflect and define your brand.

> *While experience is important, don't neglect to assess how well a candidate will fit into your company's culture.*

We try to hire associates with positive, friendly, optimistic atti-tudes because those are the feelings we want to channel to our Guests. Other companies want to project the image of exclusivity, and may hire people who are naturally more aloof. Abercrombie & Fitch hires trendy teenagers who feel at home in the clothes the store sells. Cosmetics counters typically hire attractive young women who are very conscientious about their clothing, hair, and makeup. Dis-ney hires people with positive attitudes and megawatt smiles who, like me, share a deep affinity for the company, its products, and what it does for the community.

> *Your customers may turn into your best employees.*

We hire a lot of grandmothers, moms, dads, and teenagers (who are great advocates for our brand). They are down-to-earth, friendly folks. They are salt-of-the-earth types, as wholesome as apple pie, generous, and involved in their communities. They're givers, not takers, and the reward they covet most is a satisfied Guest's smile.

A lot of our associates started out as Guests, fell in love with us, and decided they wanted to be a part of the magic we're creating. Whenever we announce the opening of a store in a new market, I always get lots of letters and e-mails from people who want to work for us because they're as passionate about what we do as I am. I always include an application, and I'm happy when they're hired. I feel like I've helped them get the job, and I consider myself lucky that they chose to work for us.

When you hire employees who share your passion for the business, you, too, will get lucky over and over again. I've seen proof that this is the right way to make hiring decisions time and time again.

Having a committed, like-minded workforce will make your job much easier.

Every day I get messages from Guests or store managers about how one of our associates stepped up to help. Sometimes the letters relate stories of excellent Guest service, or how an associate went way beyond his or her job description. Sometimes just a genuine smile or friendly demeanor will prompt these letters. Having such a committed, like-minded workforce makes my job so much easier. I know that my associates are out there doing the exact things I would if I could be in every store each day.

Take Mike Jensen, an associate in our store at Boise Towne Square in Idaho, for example. He got an offer to leave Build-A-Bear Workshop for a management job at another retailer at the mall. Though he loved working for us, Mike decided that he would have to take the other job because it was a promotion and would be better financially for him and his family.

One day before his job change, Mike stopped in at the local Wal-Mart to pick up a few things. A little girl recognized his Build-A-Bear uniform and told Mike that she loved the store. Her mom asked

Mike whether he liked working there, which sent him into an emotional tailspin. As he told the mother, he loved working for us but the next day was supposed to be his last at the company. I guess that was more than he could bear because Mike went to his supervisor the very next day and asked to stay at Build-A-Bear Workshop since he couldn't imagine a better or more rewarding job.

> *If you want employees who will choose you and your customers over a raise and promotion, hire with both your head and your heart.*

I have a feeling that Mike is going to be with us for a long time and that he has a definite future with this company. He is an asset to his store team and to the company in general, and we all look forward to watching him grow. Indeed, we have many associates in our company who are similarly motivated and committed to our Guests.

If you want employees like this, who will choose you and your customers over a raise and promotion, hire with both your head and your heart. Seek and find those people who share your passion for your products, customers, and company.

Create a Fun
Place to Work

You already know how much I love my job. I think everyone ought to look forward to Monday mornings. The good news is there are relatively simple things you can do to make sure the workweek for you and your employees begins with anticipation, not dread, and is filled with fun, not drudgery.

The idea of creating a fun, laid-back workplace really took off during the dot-com era of the late 1990s. Reporters wrote tons of articles about companies with cool decor, relaxed dress codes, and daily video game breaks. The problem was these businesses were more serious about having fun than about making a profit.

In this chapter, we'll talk about some of the ways to incorporate fun into the workday without sacrificing success. Let's begin by looking at how one company I admire does it.

Everyone ought to look forward to Monday mornings.

SAS Institute seems to make it onto every magazine's "best places to work" list. Founded in 1976, SAS is the largest privately held software company in the world with 9,500 employees worldwide and $1.5 billion in annual revenue. Employee turnover is less than 4 percent annually—an incredible statistic given that most companies struggle with turnover rates of 15 percent to 20 percent.

SAS is an incredibly fun and rewarding place to earn a paycheck. The company's corporate headquarters in Cary, North Carolina, looks and feels like one of the state's many college campuses. Trees line the 900-acre campus, and original artwork beautifies the hallways. Employees enjoy numerous generous perks and a work-life balance that is nurturing and enjoyable.

> *There are some simple things you can do to make sure each workweek begins with anticipation and fun.*

Among other things, SAS offers more than just standard benefits. Employees get unlimited sick leave. They also get three weeks of vacation, plus an extra week off between Christmas and New Year's. After 10 years, they get another week of vacation.

There's an on-site day care center that employees can enroll their kids in for a reasonable monthly fee. In addition to health insurance, SAS has a medical clinic on its campus that's open 24 hours a day for employees and their families. Workers get treatment for free; the fee for family members is nominal. The standard workweek is 35 hours, and employees are urged to leave by 5 P.M. every day.

Then there are the fun things. Two full-time artists work for the company and are responsible for creating sculptures and paintings to beautify the surroundings. Each floor of the huge headquarters building has its own break room stocked with free sodas, coffee, tea, and snacks. Fresh fruit is brought in every

Monday, breakfast treats every Friday. And there are always M&Ms—SAS spends nearly $50,000 each year on the melt-in-your-mouth candies.

The company's three cafeterias offer more than a quick meal. In one dining room, a piano player tickles the ivories, entertaining employees, while another cafeteria feels like a tropical resort with its palm tree–filled atrium.

> *The more fun people have, the harder they'll work.*

The list goes on: Employees can cash in on company-subsidized discounts for cruises, magazine subscriptions, sporting events, and products and services from local companies. They can also work out in the huge company recreation and fitness center, which includes a 10-lane swimming pool, Ping-Pong tables, pool tables, volleyball courts, basketball courts, tennis courts, soccer fields, a putting green, an aerobics center, and standard gym equipment.

As SAS demonstrates, fun seems to go hand in hand with flexibility. It's the nonmonetary rewards that help the company stand out and win kudos year after year for its work environment.

We're not nearly as big as SAS, in terms of either employee count or revenues, but we've held our own in creating a fun workplace. James Goodnight, SAS's founder and CEO, and I share a similar philosophy: "If you treat employees as if they make a difference to the company, they will make a difference to the company." And let me add this: "The more fun people have, the harder they'll work."

I previously told you about some of the unique benefits we offer at Build-A-Bear Workshop, along with my attitude toward dress codes and flexible hours. Now, let me tell you how we have fun.

> *Sometimes you need an occasional break from the ordinary to inject some fun into the workday.*

In addition to Bearemy, our fun huggable mascot, at our World Bearquarters we also have Milford. He's our Chief Executive Dog. This real-life pup of diverse background comes to work every day with his owner, Dorrie Krueger. He's a big lumbering canine who brings a lot of warmth and personality to the office. I don't feel like my workday has started until I've patted Milford on the head and gotten a sloppy kiss from him, and he puts a smile on everyone's face. After all, we obviously love furry friends of all kinds at this company!

Sometimes you just need an occasional break from the ordinary to inject some fun into the workday. Did you ever have a teacher who would take the class outside on pretty days and conduct her lessons in the sunshine? We do that sometimes at Build-A-Bear Workshop. When the sun is shining, I've seen some of our associates bring their laptops and cell phones outside and set up temporary offices beneath the biggest shade tree they can find. It's fun, it doesn't interrupt business, and it doesn't cost a thing.

> *Celebrate the special milestones in the lives of your company and employees.*

We're also a partying bunch. We celebrate birthdays, engagements, births, and other special events in our associates' lives, both at the store level and at our World Bearquarters. We sponsor group outings, like Build-A-Bear Workshop Day at St. Louis Cardinals games, and we hold weekly drawings for special gifts, movie passes, and tickets to sporting events.

These are relatively inexpensive perks to offer, but they're great fun and the payoff is a very happy, hardworking, and spirited workforce. I encourage you to keep the adage "Work hard, play hard" in mind when setting up your own shop. It's your playground, so fill it in a way that makes everyone happy.

Celebrate Mistakes
with a Red Pencil Award

Do you remember your first grade teacher? Mine was Mrs. Grace. She always wore the prettiest dresses, with a soft sweater draped around her shoulders. She was definitely more beautiful and well coiffed than your average teacher. (At least that's how I will always remember her!)

Her official job was to teach us how to read and write, but I know now that Mrs. Grace also demonstrated how to be inquisitive, confident, and speak up for yourself.

Consider rewarding employees who make the most mistakes in your company.

Mrs. Grace graded our papers with these glorious red pencils. Her pencils were long and thin, not short and stubby like ours, and sharpened to a fine point. We all coveted those incredible red No. 2s and wanted to add them to our cigar-box pencil caddies. Every week Mrs. Grace gave one red pencil away as a reward—but not to the girl who had received the best marks on her paper or the boy who'd behaved best. In Mrs. Grace's classroom, the red pencil prize went to the student who'd made the most *mistakes* that week.

Mrs. Grace encouraged us to raise our hands in class when we thought we knew an answer. It didn't matter to her if we got it wrong. If we made a mistake, in her mind, we weren't failing. We were just opening up another opportunity to learn. She didn't want the fear of being wrong to keep us from taking chances. Her only rule was that we couldn't be rewarded for making the same mistake twice.

Those red pencils soon became a status symbol in my first grade class. I was so proud of my collection. I displayed them like badges of honor in my pencil case. I never wrote with one, though, because I wanted to keep the tips as sharp as they were the day I received them.

Mrs. Grace's method was contrary to how many teachers taught in the 1950s. Two years later, my third grade teacher chastised me for asking too many questions and raising my hand too much. She even wrote a note complaining about this on my report card. Even though Mom wasn't the type to do this sort of thing, she went down to the school and told my teacher she could learn a few things from Mrs. Grace.

Why shouldn't a child in third grade be encouraged to be inquisitive? Why should she be afraid of getting the answer wrong? Why should anyone?

> *Mistakes are merely part of the learning process.*

Being in Mrs. Grace's classroom changed my life. She taught me it's okay to take risks. Through her, I learned you shouldn't fear mistakes, but rather embrace them and learn from them. I still follow those rules today.

As a result, I don't have the same perspective on failure that a lot of people have. I look at mistakes as being part of the learning process.

My early days of retailing also taught me that mistakes were just fine, and could prove to be rather rewarding. When I first started out, we used to mark down the prices on merchandise using a red pencil, very much like the ones I coveted from Mrs. Grace. Those red pencil marks on the price tags indicated a mistake. The store had too much inventory that it couldn't sell at full price. But retailers plan for these kinds of things. We had a "mistake budget," and a certain amount of money was allocated for markdowns. It was all right to make mistakes.

I try to impart this same philosophy to the people I work with. When they come to our World Bearquarters for training, I tell new store managers about Mrs. Grace and give each of them a red pencil. That's their license to take risks and try new things without fear of failure or management's judgment. It's kind of like the "Get Out of Jail Free" card in Monopoly®.

We also give out a special Red Pencil Award in our company. To win it, you have to make a mistake—or what most people would perceive as a mistake—that really turns out to be a better way of doing business, saves the company money, or turns into a new product. I try to encourage people to take risks and to make the most of the mistakes that do occur.

People always ask me about the mistakes we've made at Build-A-Bear Workshop. It's really hard for me to recall any, because, as you know, I don't think mistakes are bad. In my book, they make you better. We've taken some of our old so-called "mistakes" and turned them into the normal course of business.

> *Give workers license to take risks without fear of failure or management's wrath.*

As just one example, we like to give our Guests brightly colored ribbons to tie around the ears of their huggable animals. One day, our ribbon vendor sent us the wrong width—a quarter-inch wide instead of an inch wide. Rather than fussing about the mix-up, an associate at our Saint Louis Galleria store, Sherry Manuso, tied the ribbon into little hair bows using a rubber band to the ears of our girl bears. Guests loved them, so we ordered more of the narrower ribbon and kept making these bows. The mistake of the wrong ribbon being shipped to us turned out to be a really good thing. It gave us yet another way to add value to the overall experience.

Much later it dawned on me that we were making another mistake with this. We didn't have to make those bows ourselves. One of our vendors could do it for us, freeing up associates to interact with Guests more and to think of other creative ways to improve the business.

I made a similar mistake in designing the clothing for our bears. When I was ordering clothes from our manufacturer, I didn't think to ask them to leave a little hole in the back of each outfit so the animal's tail could fit through. Once the clothes arrived in the store, our associates started making these peekaboo holes by ripping an inch out of the seam of every outfit. When I realized my mistake, I didn't beat myself up. I just called our manufacturer and asked for a tiny hole opening the seam in every outfit. Problem solved!

Encourage people to try new things.

I actually allow myself to make mistakes, and I try to be tolerant of them in others. When an employee gets something wrong, it's human nature for the supervisor to be upset and demand that the worker fix it. But people don't make mistakes on purpose. Everyone really wants to do things right, though nobody is perfect. And what's the harm in excusing the mistakes we all make—or in simply trying them out to see if what seems to be a misfit really does work?

Just as we were preparing to open our first store, I received a shipment of product from our manufacturer. To my dismay, one batch of bears was the wrong color—about two shades lighter than it was supposed to be. I didn't want to use these stuffed animals because we planned to display the bears against a light-colored wall, and I feared their pale fur wouldn't show up well against that background.

Because we were so close to opening, we needed to put something in that empty space. So, I displayed the miscolored bears there, intending to replace them as soon as the manufacturer could get the right color to us.

Those butterscotch-colored bears turned out to be our top seller! We ultimately had to ask our manufacturer to make numerous additional batches.

> *Experiment freely, and view every so-called mistake as one step closer to getting things right.*

I hope we continue to make more mistakes worthy of Mrs. Grace's red pencil, so we can all learn the lessons we need to make our company more successful. I encourage you to do the same. Experiment freely, and view every so-called mistake as one step closer to getting things just right.

"With great power comes great responsibility."

That's what the fictional Peter Parker's uncle, Ben, told him as he matured from a normal teenage boy into Spider-Man.

I don't have the life-and-death responsibilities of a superhero. But as the founder and top bear of a publicly traded company, I hold quite a bit of responsibility for our associates, Guests, and shareholders. In addition to making money, it's up to me to create a good working environment where people are encouraged to contribute and feel valued for those contributions.

As the head of your company, you hold a lot of responsibility for your employees, customers, and investors.

Like every corporate leader, I'm ultimately responsible for building a company that people work for because they *want* to, not because they *have* to. There are lots of ways to create this kind of atmosphere, like giving associates flexible work schedules and making the setting fun—all things I previously discussed.

But developing a healthy and hospitable work environment is rooted in respect.

You must treat the people around you respectfully. I think that's one of the critical differences between being a "boss" and being a "leader."

Bosses are in charge. They are dictatorial. Their word is law.

Leaders are heaped with the same responsibilities and pressures as bosses, but they don't behave the same way. They realize the value of their team members. They listen to what their employees have to say. They create a climate of reciprocal respect, not fear.

You must admit that the Golden Rule is a good one: Do unto others as you would have them do unto you. At Build-A-Bear Workshop, our bearish version of that is, "Give honey unto others as you would have honey given unto you."

> *Create a company where people work for you because they <u>want</u> to, not because they <u>have</u> to.*

Would you want to be yelled at? Would you want to be beaten up verbally for every mistake you ever made? Would you want to be dressed down in front of a coworker or customer? Of course not. So, why treat others like that?

I like to think of myself as a collaborative leader, but not a particularly great manager. In fact, my pure management skills have probably deteriorated as I've moved up through the ranks of corporate America to lead my own company. My days are longer and my personal time has taken a backseat to building this enterprise. But I have a lot of energy, a good brain for problem solving, and a clear vision for how to make Build-A-Bear Workshop successful. I also know how to coach people to reach their full potential and make the biggest possible contribution they can while also helping the business.

I don't go into our stores dressed like a chief executive officer. I leave my business attire at home and instead wear my Bear Builder clothes—khaki pants, a denim shirt with our logo, red vest, and my sneakers—so I can get right to work with our associates. When they see me dressed that way and doing their same job, they know that I respect them and the work they do. I have the opportunity to coach them through different situations and model how we should treat our Guests.

I believe that people come to work every day to make a contribution. I know I do. Even while working for someone else, I always felt most productive when it was clear that the job I did made a difference to the company and our customers. Employees like to feel valuable at work and know that they are appreciated.

> **Bosses** *are in charge and dictatorial*. **Leaders** *listen to what their employees have to say and create a climate of reciprocal respect.*

It's amazing how much hard work a person can deliver when they feel this way. Countless worker satisfaction surveys show employees perform at their best when they feel appreciated and recognized. It's not about the paycheck!

I'm not advocating that you hand out false praise to employees in order to con them into working harder. That is not respectful, and you're not adhering to the Golden Rule if you're lying or being deceptive. But if you do right by your employees—reward them with praise, encourage their participation, and offer criticism that is instructive, not insulting—you'll also do right by your company.

I once heard a store manager compliment an employee on the great job she'd done that week selling cashmere sweaters, and then ask, "How can we sell more cotton sweaters next week?"

> *Follow the Golden Rule: Do unto others as you would have them do unto you.*

That manager had mastered respectful leadership. Sales of cashmere sweaters had been strong, the manager was telling her, but sales of cotton sweaters were disappointing and he expected better numbers from her the following week. He praised the employee for something she'd done well and challenged her to use her talents to improve sales in another area.

As a leader in your company, your words have incredible weight. Why not make them more motivating than demoralizing? More energizing than deflating? The difference often is in the delivery. It bears repeating: You really have to be mindful about what you say to employees—and *how* you say it.

I visit our stores every week, and sometimes see things that don't reflect the image we want to present to our Guests. Maybe there's dust on the floor. Perhaps someone is in the back room talking on a cell phone instead of interacting with Guests. Occasionally the lines are too long, or some bear bins may be close to empty.

> *Coach people to reach their full potential and make the biggest contribution possible.*

My ultimate goal is to fix these problems, but not at the expense of associate morale. If I were a dictatorial *boss*, instead of a respectful *leader*, I might yell or throw a fit about those things. That would certainly scare store associates into getting things right. But it's not my style, and it's not a very effective way to run a business these days.

I believe the era of the dictatorial boss has passed, and that people choose to work (and work hard) for those they admire—thoughtful and respectful leaders in a more collaborative way.

A few years back, a fellow manager from our World Bearquarters and I visited one of our better-performing stores. Comparable store sales, a key figure used by retailers to measure success, were through the roof. I had to see what made this particular Build-A-Bear Workshop store such a star performer.

When I got there, I realized it wasn't so perfect after all. Sure, the sales figures were impressive, but apparently this was happening at the expense of the Guest experience. The store had a new manager, who had come to work for us from a big-box retailer, and the place was an absolute mess. The merchandise displays looked junky. The bins we keep our stuffed animals in were all jumbled. Cats were keeping company with the dogs, for goodness' sake. Some clothing and accessory racks were empty. It was a real nightmare!

> *Employees like to feel valuable at work and know they are appreciated. It's not just about the paycheck!*

Somehow, I kept my disappointment at bay. I walked in with my team members and introduced myself. "What can we do to help?" I asked in the next breath. "It looks like you could use some assistance restocking the shelves." We put down our briefcases and brought stock out into the store. We got to work putting it on the shelves and racks.

Once the flow of Guests slowed, we left for about a half-hour to let the manager and his associates finish the job of restocking. When we returned, however, we found the store was still pretty much like we'd left it—still a lot of work to be done.

When we talked about it later, the store manager told me he wasn't used to our style of leadership and didn't grasp our sense of urgency. Neither of us had yelled, as his big-box bosses would have done, so he didn't realize we wanted the shelves restocked and the displays neatened, as we immediately tried to show him.

> *As a company leader, realize the impact your words and actions have on everyone else.*

Despite the invitation to do so, we didn't go off half-cocked and berate the manager for his mistakes. We realized instead that he needed more help to acclimate to the Build-A-Bear Workshop culture and our way of doing things. The district manager began visiting the store more often—not to check up on things, but to help the new manager by making constructive suggestions and coaching him through any difficulties.

We knew this man had a contribution to make to our company, and we understood that the best way to engender that contribution was to treat him as a valued, respected member of our team. We praised him for his successes, listened to his suggestions, worked alongside him, and offered him help when needed.

I would want the same thing for myself and can guarantee your employees will appreciate that from you as well.

One of the best things you can do in business is listen to those who work for you. And I mean *really* listen.

Build-A-Bear Workshop has thousands of associates around the world, and every one has the boss's ear. From their first day on the job, our associates are invited to contact me with any questions, concerns, or ideas they have.

I can't understand why more executives fail to make themselves more easily accessible to their employees. When you don't, you're missing out on so much—including a direct connection to your customers and a tremendous source of ideas that might boost your brand, save you money, and improve sales.

Listen to those who work for you.

Lots of companies have suggestion boxes, where employees can submit their concerns, questions, and brainstorms. But few of these

99

find their way to the people with the authority to make change happen. I really do read every single e-mail I receive from our associates. I'd be foolish not to. As you know, some of our best ideas have come from them.

Having an open line of communication between our stores and our World Bearquarters in Saint Louis is just one way we empower associates to contribute at Build-A-Bear Workshop.

Employees, particularly those who work directly with customers, are the brain trust of every company. You ought to call on them every time there's a problem that needs to be solved. Smart companies aren't afraid to bring in outside help when it's needed. They'll hire marketing firms, information technology (IT) consultants, lawyers, and accountants for their expertise. But if you're smart, you'll look inward for expertise, too.

In our company, the best consultants are our associates. Part of the reason we've able to do this is because they have a lot of autonomy and are encouraged to try new and creative things (remember the red pencil?) without fear of being reprimanded for a mistake or wrong move.

> *Make yourself easily accessible to employees. Otherwise, you'll miss a direct connection to your customers and a tremendous source of ideas.*

In June 2005, we added a pink flamingo to our collection of stuffed animals. We encouraged our store associates to be creative in celebrating the launch of this new product. One store in Chandler, Arizona, really made the flamingos fly off the shelves with a simple, interactive experience for Guests. The staff hung up a poster that looked like a front yard and bought flamingo stickers from a local craft store. Anybody who made a flamingo got to put a sticker on the poster and write his or her name beside it. By the end of the weekend, that poster was full of flamingo stickers. The poster also helped to extend the interactive experience for each Guest who bought a pink flamingo. It was so much fun and so successful, we plan to adapt this same idea for future promotions!

There are countless examples like this in our company. When I was in New York for the opening of our Build-A-Bear Workshop store on Fifth Avenue, I also visited our sister "friends 2B made" store. Associates had Guests pick a heart and put it in an envelope with their doll's personality traits—a unique part of shaping who your doll will be. Then they'd shake up the envelope to infuse the heart with those traits. That was a great idea, and it's something our other "friends 2B made" stores now use.

I was lucky enough to witness these great associate ideas in action during store visits, though I can't be at every location all the time. That's why we've developed processes to channel the expertise and successes of our individual stores and associates.

We have Breakthrough Operations Bears (BOBS) committees. We select our best-performing stores to take part in these committees, which hold brainstorming and planning sessions for the entire company.

> *Employees are the brain trust of every company.*

We've used BOBS for a variety of purposes, and give an array of people the opportunity to participate. We've called together Bear Builder associates who get high Guest satisfaction ratings to share how they do their jobs. Store managers who get a lot of Build-A-Party celebration bookings share their secrets of success and help develop best practices for the entire company. When we're preparing to launch a new stuffed animal, like the flamingo, we call on those stores that have had the most successful launch results in the past to help us in planning. When we want to increase the sales of shoes, we gather together those stores that have recorded the most shoe sales and ask them how they did it.

I'm glad I don't have to think of all these things by myself. There's no way I could. I also believe that when you empower employees to contribute, you position your company to be more successful.

When employees have a hand in developing new products, ideas, and processes, there's greater buy-in among the workforce. If Sharon knows that her coworker Steve was involved in creating the company's new marketing program, she's more likely to accept that it will be effective. She won't view it as an edict or the latest whim from the corporate ivory tower. And those practices based on employee input are likely to work better, too, because they're developed from a frontline perspective.

Learning from your own employees is something every company should do.

At Build-A-Bear Workshop, we like to hire those who have worked at other great businesses we respect and admire, like the Gap, the Limited, and restaurants like the Cheesecake Factory. That way we can find out what insights and lessons they gathered while working there.

Ask those you hire this question: "What are we not doing that your previous employer did?"

Most people take that as an invitation to stroke your ego. They'll start talking about why they hated working for their former company and tell you why yours is so much better. They think that's what you want to hear. But it's not what I want to hear.

> *When you empower employees to contribute, you position your company to be more successful.*

I don't hire people to stroke my ego, and I'm not looking to uplift Build-A-Bear Workshop by listening to a litany of complaints about other companies. I want to learn from these associates. I'm not interested in bringing on people who hated their last job. I want to hire those who loved where they worked and came to us with great habits and ideas they learned on the job.

When you use this technique with your employees, you may have to ask the question multiple times in varied ways. But once you explain what you're looking for—concrete ideas and not complaints—people will offer insights and examples that you'll be able to use in your business.

We are a young, fast-growing company. Sometimes the obvious ideas are not that obvious. For instance, one of our managers told us how his old company used to have district meetings where managers got together monthly to share ideas and get to know one another. We had a national managers' meeting once a year, but no other regular, face-to-face opportunities for store managers to interact. Thanks to his suggestion, that has changed. We may not have them monthly, but weekly calls and quarterly meetings bring our teams together. It's a good idea for both employees and the company to have managers working together in the same region interact and share ideas on a regular basis.

> *Ask new hires what you're not doing that their previous employer did that could make their jobs easier and the company more successful.*

I'm thankful for the wisdom that employee brought from his previous company. You have an incredible brain trust within the ranks of your business as well. Listen to what those around you have to say, and use their insights to make your company even better.

Know What You Don't Know

What you *don't* know could fill a book.

Some might take that as a scathing insult. To me, it's a compliment.

I know what I don't know, and I'm much smarter and more successful for it.

When I was a little girl, I embraced the fact that I didn't know everything. I'd go scurrying to my parents, my teachers, or the encyclopedia in search of the answers to life's great mysteries. I've never been afraid to raise my hand or ask questions—a legacy of Mrs. Grace. I always want the correct answer, even if that means asking what may appear to be a stupid question.

Don't feel like you have to do everything alone.

When you go into business for yourself, it's important to understand what your expertise is and all that you are able to do by yourself. But it's equally important to know what your weaknesses are so you can get help in those areas.

Don't feel like you have to do everything all alone. And don't shy away from asking questions because you're afraid of sounding dumb or seeming less business-savvy than you fancy yourself to be. The question you *don't* ask of your lawyer, accountant, or insurance agent could really hurt your business. And that's just plain dumb.

When I bought insurance to cover Build-A-Bear Workshop, I didn't ask all the right questions. That ended up being a big mistake.

Around Thanksgiving during our first year in business (and our first month in operation), the roof of the warehouse where we stored our entire inventory caved in. It was a four-story building. We were on the second floor, and the third and fourth floors came crashing down into our space. While no one was injured, everything we had stored there was destroyed in an instant.

This experience underscores how ignorance—not being aware of all you don't know—can hurt your business. Though I'd been in retail for more than 25 years, I wasn't savvy about business insurance. It's a lesson I learned only after the roof came crashing down.

I insured the business the way you might insure your home. We were able to recoup the cost of the lost inventory from our insurance company, but didn't have a policy to protect us against the interruption in business that the roof collapse caused. We didn't have business interruption insurance, and we needed it.

> *The question you <u>don't</u> ask of experts can really hurt your business.*

Though it was a royal headache at the time, I'm actually glad the roof caved in in 1997 and not 2006. Otherwise, we might still be underinsured. If we didn't have business interruption insurance today, a disaster at our warehouse and distribution center would be a calamity. Our operations would grind to a halt, crippling our stores, and we'd receive no remuneration for this.

We've already had cause to make a claim against our business interruption policy. A fire at a mall put one of our stores out of business for two weeks. But we lost no revenue because we were protected by the appropriate insurance. Hurricane Katrina caused our store in New Orleans to be closed for more than a month.

I tell you this in case insurance is one of those areas in which you don't have a lot of expertise. You're not alone. Most of us know little about this subject and its many intricacies. Take my advice: Consider buying business interruption insurance. Work with a skilled broker who can help you explore all the coverage options for your particular business. It's the unexpected things—like a roof caving in—that you don't think about ahead of time, but that can cause you tremendous trouble if you're caught unprepared.

You might not bring as much experience to the table in your new endeavor as I did when I started Build-A-Bear Workshop. That's the first "don't know" you have to address. Before writing your business plan, get experience in that industry. If you dream of opening your own restaurant, I don't know how you can possibly do it successfully unless you've spent some time working in a restaurant. Every industry has its own unique rules and ins and outs, things you can't possibly know about unless you've experienced them firsthand or done copious amounts of research. In the restaurant business, for example, you need to understand how your waitstaff is to be paid, the art of estimating how much food to buy, and which local health codes you will be subject to.

> *Consider business interruption insurance in case a disaster forces you to temporarily shut your doors.*

Though I was experienced in the retail business, I'd never run a business like Build-A-Bear Workshop before. I had just visited numerous factories overseas, but I had to learn about the toy business and pay closer attention to how teddy bears are made. Before, I'd always had a corporate headquarters full of experts to help me. With Build-A-Bear Workshop, I had to do my own market research. In the very beginning, I even had to figure out the finances for myself. I certainly had had experience in selling my business ideas to corporate leadership, but was inexperienced at pitching a business to bankers.

There was plenty I didn't know, and I turned to a variety of resources to boost my knowledge. I downloaded the annual reports of companies I admired and read them to learn more about how public company finances work. I read books, like those I mentioned earlier, to learn how to write a business plan. I studied web sites that offer advice for entrepreneurs. (Two I'd recommend are the U.S. Small Business Administration at www.sba.com and *Inc.* magazine at www.inc.com/guides, which indexes a large collection of business how-to articles covering topics such as setting up an office, grassroots marketing, creating a web site, finding a mentor, raising start-up capital, buying a franchise, and creating a tax strategy.)

That research phase was fun. After all, I read *The World Book Encyclopedia* for fun as a kid. I was also a journalism major in college, so digging into things is in my blood.

Other people can help fill in what you don't know.

> *Before writing your business plan, get experience in your chosen industry.*

One of my retail mentors, who wanted me to be careful that I didn't overextend myself financially in the early days of Build-A-Bear Workshop, told me that I didn't need a chief financial officer (CFO). But I knew that I didn't know nearly enough to handle the complex finances of this growing business by myself, even when it was small. I also understood that I required more than just an accountant who would occasionally manage the books. I needed a full-time person in that role, and I hired Tina Klocke, who remains the company's Chief Financial Bear (CFB—bearspeak for chief financial officer) today.

You must realize when it's time to hire someone to help you out, either as an employee or on a contract basis. If you can't navigate your way around a tax return, don't attempt to. Hire someone to do your taxes for you. Business returns are infinitely more complicated than personal ones.

If you find it difficult to write a coherent sentence, hire a wordsmith to churn out your press releases or retain an outside agency to do that work. If you have trouble booting your computer, outsource your information technology needs to someone skilled in the field.

Recognize your strengths and weaknesses with equal candor and outsource those things you can't possibly handle on your own. Doing so will make the business stronger.

Understand that one expert might not know everything you need to properly operate your business. Tina Klocke is an excellent CFB, but when she joined the company she didn't have experience in helping a start-up raise money. Fortunately, two of our investors, Wayne Smith and Barney Ebsworth of Windsor Capital, did. I relied on them to fill in those areas where Tina and I were lacking. Wayne, in particular, was very knowledgeable about the finances of start-up companies, and he really helped us devise strategies and negotiate how best to raise capital.

> *Don't rely on your family lawyer for business advice. Find a specialist in the subject at hand.*

I know that when many people go into business, they consult their family lawyer for advice. Even if that lawyer is a whiz at keeping your grandmother's will out of probate, he or she may not have the skills to help with your professional legal affairs. In fact, you may discover that you need to seek the advice and services of many attorneys because business law is such a vast and specialized field. You may need to consult different attorneys for advice on Internet operations, trademarks and trade secrets, incorporation and partnerships, employment issues, contracts, mergers and acquisitions, real estate matters, and raising capital.

Never be afraid to ask for help.

It's often said that a man will never ask for directions, but a woman will. I won't weigh in on that age-old debate of the sexes. But I will say this: I am never afraid to ask for directions, and you shouldn't be afraid to ask for the help you need to make your business even better.

Seek the Help of Outside Experts

As you know by now, I'm big supporter of teamwork. I can't do everything by myself. I know I need other people to help. Even in writing this book, I sought help from a writer, a book developer, and a publisher—all of whom are experienced experts in producing business titles.

You sometimes have to seek help from outsiders to supplement your in-house resources.

In business, you sometimes have to seek help from outsiders to supplement the resources of your team. There are all kinds of reasons for contracting the services of outside experts. You'll gain access to high-level expertise in areas beyond your core competencies. You'll get an unbiased assessment of your business. Without hiring extra full-time employees, you can boost staffing levels for special projects. In the long run, you may even save money.

Build-A-Bear Workshop retains numerous consultants to help the business run better and more efficiently. Some of these contractor relationships are pretty standard for our industry. Others buck conventional practice, yet work well for us.

For example, even as we've grown to more than 200 stores, we've continued to outsource our real estate and construction management function. When planning our first store, we entered into a partnership with Hycel Properties Company of Saint Louis. At that time, Hycel owned the Saint Louis Galleria, where we opened the first of our expanding roster of stores. After our success at the mall, we contracted with Hycel to find high-traffic and high-profile locations for our other stores and to manage the construction of these locations.

> *Think about your core competencies when deciding what to take on yourself, and what to farm out to the experts.*

At the time, economics and inexperience dictated that this was the best way for us to go. Scouting retail locations and negotiating leases is a complicated job. It wasn't a core competency of mine, so I had to look outside my own company for expertise. I suppose I could have created an internal real estate department and hired someone to head that up, but in the beginning there wasn't enough work to justify a full-time position. Plus, I was focused on keeping our corporate infrastructure as small as possible, so we could spend our money on building the brand.

We certainly have enough stores and growth now to justify an internal real estate and construction department. We're constantly searching for new places to open stores. At any given time, we probably have 10 to 15 under construction, and another 10 to 15 in lease negotiation.

But we've decided to continue the relationship with Hycel because we have come to depend on their expertise and efficiency. Besides, I don't think I could hire a staff of people who would do as good a job for the same price, or be as dedicated.

> *Sometimes outside experts may eventually become part of your staff.*

Hycel's construction management division, in particular, is well worth the cost. We'd have to employ several staffers at considerable expense to do the job they do for a reasonable monthly fee.

Hycel sold its stake in the Saint Louis Galleria and now offers its services to other retail companies. I am proud to refer other up-and-coming retail businesses to Hycel. Real estate scouting and leasing is time-consuming and complex. It pays to let an expert handle that. Hycel, in partnership with our Strategic Planning Bear, does a really good job of finding the right spaces and negotiating the right lease terms for us, so we can focus on what we do best—creating an outstanding Guest experience.

You really need to think about your core competencies—those things you do best—when deciding what work to take on yourself and what to farm out to the experts. When writing your business plan, clearly identify your strengths and weaknesses, and come up with a game plan for covering any deficiencies. Pay someone else to help you in those areas where you lack knowledge or need supplemental help.

For example, even though my background is in marketing, I hired the Adrienne Weiss Company, a branding consultant I'd worked with before, to help build a brand around my vision. The company specializes in this kind of work, and I knew the investment would be worthwhile. Adrienne also helped us develop our doll concept, "friends 2B made."

In 2003, after extensive research on our brand and our Guests using Parthenon Group out of Boston, we hired Barkley Evergreen &

Partners, an advertising and marketing firm in Kansas City, Missouri, to assist in our marketing effort and to help develop a national brand campaign.

And although we keep a detailed database of where our Guests live, we have contracted with demographics companies to help us find and target our primary customer base.

> *Part of the value outsiders bring to your business is an unbiased viewpoint, with fresh ideas and legitimate criticisms.*

Sometimes outside experts may eventually become part of your staff. That's what happened with Jill Saunders, who ran her own small public relations (PR) firm. We initially retained Jill's company to write press releases and coordinate media coverage for our business. As our publicity efforts grew along with the company, we brought Jill on board as a full-time associate to lead our PR department.

We still occasionally seek the help of other public relations agencies when we need to supplement our own resources. Specifically, these agencies help us publicize our charitable programs (such as Stuffed With Hugs) and big events like the opening of our huge New York City store. But Jill and her team are full-time Build-A-Bear Workshop associates.

Scott Adams, who draws the comic strip *Dilbert*, often makes fun of consultants as ineffectual puppets of upper management. I know that some executives hire consultants and outside experts only to bolster their own viewpoints or to seek validation of their business decisions. That's a terrible reason for entering into a relationship with a consultant or contractor. Part of the value that outsiders bring to your business is an unbiased viewpoint. They have fresh ideas, and they may have worthy criticisms you should heed.

My friend Adrienne Weiss tells me people have paid her hundreds of thousands of dollars for her services, yet haven't always implemented her ideas and suggestions. If you're not willing to listen to what your outside experts say—and act on their advice—you're wasting money and keeping your business from moving forward.

> *Contract with people who are truly experts at what they do. Make sure they are trustworthy and understand your company's culture.*

That said, choose the outsiders you decide to work with wisely. Contract with people who are truly experts at what they do. That way they'll add value to your business instead of wasting your money. When Build-A-Bear Workshop seeks outside help, we develop task-specific requests for proposals. We carefully review the proposals and ultimate deliverables that these experts send us and identify the best person or company to work on that particular project.

When hiring outsiders, make sure they become part of your team and understand your company's culture. To make the most of the relationship, you'll likely have to share confidential and proprietary information with them. (They'll need as much information as possible to help your business.) If you feel you can't do that, you don't have the right partner.

You can pay for outside help several ways, though it's usually on a per-project basis or through a monthly retainer. Whatever method you choose, make sure that both you and the consultant understand the terms and expectations of the contract. Review invoices as they come in—and before checks are written. Schedule frequent reviews to make sure your goals and the agreed-to deliverables are being met and to revise objectives as necessary.

Make the terms with outside consultants clear by demanding a written agreement.

My philosophy when paying someone for outside services is that I'm going to get the most I can out of them. Find the right person or business to do the work, share all you can to help them accomplish their job, and regularly review their work to ensure that everything is going as you expected.

Keep Score

W hen I was in elementary school, my teacher assigned me to write a book report on the Edgar Allan Poe story, *The Black Cat*. I really wanted to impress the teacher and get a good grade, so I asked my mother to help me with the report. I didn't want her to do the whole report, as some kids requested of their parents. I only wanted her to help me draw the cover because she was artistic and I knew she'd do a better job than I ever could.

> *In business, as in school, you must find ways to measure employees' performance and reward them for a job well done.*

I was surprised when my mother told me to do my own homework. She said she did hers when she was a kid, and I needed to do mine, too. Boy, did that make me mad! But I pressed on, sulkily writing the report and drawing the cover illustration all by myself. As frustrated as I was then, I have to admit that my mother, as she always had a tendency to be, was right about making me do my own work. The teacher gave me an A+ on the book report. But more than the grade, I cherished the comment she wrote on it: "Great cover!"

Believe it or not, that book report is one of my most prized possessions. I still have it in my basement, boxed up with other keepsakes. Why, you ask? Because it's meaningful and a real confidence booster to be recognized for your hard work—not to mention that my teacher's praise inspired me to try to do other great work. My mother, as usual, was right.

> *When you get a letter of praise concerning an employee, pass it around as a way of motivating others.*

In business, as in school, you need to find ways to measure employees' performance and reward them for a job well done. Financials are pretty easy to track. Any serious business likely already monitors the ups and downs of its revenues, profits, and expenses, and each employee's contribution to those numbers. But I think a worker's report card should be more extensive than this. Specifically, employees should be graded on how well they treat customers and rewarded when they do a particularly good job.

While most companies give out bonuses based on sales performance and growth, we take a different approach. We give out financial bonuses based on our Guests' happiness. Each store has to achieve a certain Guest satisfaction score each month. Otherwise, neither the store manager nor the associates at that location receive a bonus.

Gauging customer satisfaction levels isn't as hard to do as you might think. As I've already mentioned, our Guests write to us all the time. When we get a letter or e-mail praising a particular store or associate, we pass it around the company, up and down the chain of command. Our goal is to provide a constant stream of praise and good examples. This has proven to be incredibly effective in motivating our associates. We've found that they like being involved in setting standards of service for their coworkers, and they also like following good examples set by others. In our experience, positive reinforcement certainly works much better than criticism.

> *Positive reinforcement works much better than criticism.*

If an associate does something super special—and this happens all the time—we'll reward them with lots of fanfare and hoopla. We gush over them like grandmas do over their newborn grandchildren. Exemplary associates get honored with a tin of brownies or big bouquet of cookies, which we always have delivered when the store is busy and Guests are around. We want our Guests to share in the celebration, and we want them to know just how seriously we take their happiness. These tokens of appreciation don't cost much, but they send a clear signal to associates that their work is valued. I challenge you to find your own unique way of rewarding your best workers. Be sure to make it fun, loud, and attention grabbing.

We also track Guest satisfaction through telephone and online surveys. When I was at Payless ShoeSource, I was proud to see in our sales reports that one of every six pairs of shoes sold in America was bought in one of our stores. Still, that doesn't compare to the pride I feel when I get our weekly results now and see that Guest satisfaction is through the roof.

Every Guest who makes a purchase receives a cash register receipt that gives instructions on how to participate in the survey. "Did we make you smile?" is one of the questions, and it's a primary benchmark of a store's success. If the answer to that question is "no," we want to know why and figure out what we can do to fix it. Again, bonuses are tied to these scores and managers post the store's weekly report cards so associates can see them. Posting the grades accomplishes several things. It shows associates what areas of Guest service, if any, they're neglecting as a group. The scores, if they're good, give our associates something to be proud of and strive for in the future. Again, it's positive reinforcement.

> *Tie bonuses to both individual achievement and group performance.*

Notice that I speak of group performance when talking about the weekly Guest satisfaction surveys. We don't post individual scores on the bulletin board. Doing so would be an incredibly bad idea. There's nothing wrong with holding up an employee who does a great job as an example. But a good boss should never castigate an employee in public or use his or her mistake or failure as an example. Such behavior is demeaning—not instructive or motivational. In fact, it is likely to lower the morale of the entire group. If you need to point out an employee's flaws or poor performance, save those discussions for behind closed doors. It's one example of our red pencil philosophy in action.

> *Never castigate an employee in public or use his or her mistake or failure as an example.*

Throughout this chapter, I've talked about ways to keep score in business. I hope you understand there's another side to that coin as well. When you keep score, you have to offer a prize to the winners. Think about baseball. Teams keep score all year long, not for the heck of it, but because they want the big prize—the World Series

Championship. In our business, unlike in baseball or a beauty pageant, we don't want just one winner in the Guest service competition. We want to celebrate *everyone's* hard work, and that's why we've designated September as Bear Builder Appreciation Month. It's our official way of paying tribute to the associates who are the reason for our success all year round. We give out awards and honor associates with gifts and paid days off. At our World Bearquarters, we also schedule company picnics and group outings, like to a St. Louis Cardinals game.

In addition, we advertise to our Guests that September is a special month at Build-A-Bear Workshop and encourage them to participate by honoring their favorite Bear Builder.

October is We Appreciate Managers (WAM) Month and similar celebrations are held for our store management teams. We give our Guests a reason to visit our stores again while at the same time making our associates feel extra special. (Savvy marketing, don't you think?)

> *Let customers be a part of your employee appreciation efforts.*

There's no reason that every business couldn't follow our lead and designate an employee appreciation month. This is a great way to boost morale and say thank you to your employees in a very tangible way. If you follow these methods for keeping score, everyone will be a winner.

Read, Act, and Share

My regular trips to the library are among my fondest memories from childhood. I enjoyed being able to take a new book home each week and I savored the experience of learning more about the world on every page.

I've always loved the feeling of getting lost in a book, so engrossed in the plot and the characters that you can't put it down until you reach the final page. Even now, when I have the luxury of a lazy afternoon, I usually spend it wrapped up in a warm blanket thumbing through the pages of a great book.

A lending library is an easy and inexpensive way to offer professional development to your employees.

I still have an insatiable taste for fiction, and usually the fluffier the better. But as I've grown older, my tastes have expanded, and I now read a lot of nonfiction as well. I'm drawn to business books that tell the stories of great companies. I've probably read every book that has ever been published about Walt Disney and his company, and my copy of Starbucks chairman and CEO Howard Schultz's *Pour Your Heart into It* (Hyperion, 1997) is dog-eared and worn because I've read it so many times and marked up so many important passages. My focus on finding the best in other companies came from one of my all-time favorites, *In Search of Excellence* by Tom Peters (Harper & Row, 1982).

I always feel smarter after reading a really good book, and often learn things that I can then apply to my own business. The best books make me think, and I regularly recommend those that were especially beneficial to my friends and business associates. I also refer them to the countless Guests and aspiring entrepreneurs who write to me asking for advice.

One day it struck me that if I'm learning so much from these books, I bet our associates could benefit from them as well. That was the inspiration for setting up a lending library at our World Bearquarters in Saint Louis. When I finish with a business book I've purchased, I put it on the shelf at the office. Associates can then check these books out and keep them for as long as they like. They're also encouraged to stock the shelves with books they've finished and found to be helpful. Our little library has grown quite significantly since we started it and now includes books from our favorite authors on a variety of topics, including entrepreneurship, customer service, inspirational businesses, teamwork, management techniques, history, marketing, and leadership.

To be a great boss, you must ensure that your employees are being given regular opportunities to learn and grow. One way to accomplish this is by setting up a similar lending library within your company. Stock it with books (like this one, I hope) that you found helpful as you were building your business. Also include books that are specific to your industry and that contain career-building techniques your employees will find useful. Encourage everyone to check out these books and add their own favorite titles to the selection. Over time, you'll be amazed how beneficial this will be to the well-being of everyone at the company—not to mention your bottom line.

> *By reading other business books, workers will gain better insight into your company and their jobs.*

A lending library is an easy and inexpensive way to offer employees professional development by providing them with texts and tools that will help them do their jobs better. When associates browse and read the books in our library, I think they gain better insight into my own personal business philosophies and how those translate to their roles at Build-A-Bear Workshop. For example, you'll find a lot of books about customer service and much-loved companies in our library. Though I say it a million times a day, it never hurts to underscore that making Guests happy is our number one priority. These books do just that.

I still love roaming the stacks of the library and pulling new books off the shelf. Each one holds the promise of new knowledge, and I never know where I'm going to find inspiration or my next idea. So, I continue reading, acting on what I read, and sharing what I've read. I hope you'll do the same.

Part Three

Connecting with Your Customers

See Yourself Through the Public's Eyes

Among the best ways to get inside the mind of your customers is to act like one.

Every week, I travel around the country visiting our stores. Quite often, I don't show up as Maxine Clark, Chief Executive Bear. Instead of introducing myself as the founder of the company, I walk through the doors and pretend to be a regular Guest. When associates greet me, I act as if this is the first time, instead of the millionth, I've ever walked into a Build-A-Bear Workshop store. I let them engage me as I go through the process of making my own furry friend. I choose clothing and accessories for my animal, fill out a birth certificate, and pay for my purchase at the cash register (although the manager usually discovers me by then).

The best way to learn about your business is by becoming a customer and looking at yourself through the public's eyes.

I make these incognito visits not so I can spy on our associates, but so I can experience our company as our Guests do. It's always an eye-opening adventure. Sometimes, I discover problems or things that we ought to be doing better. Most times, I feel incredibly validated when I see just how well we're treating Guests and executing on our promise to make a visit to Build-A-Bear Workshop a fun and memorable one.

No matter what your industry, there's so much you can learn from being a customer of your own business. You'll gain a new, enlightened perspective when you start looking at yourself through your customer's eyes.

Today, Build-A-Bear Workshop has more than 200 stores worldwide, so it's easier for me to go unrecognized. I realize not everyone can do that, but that's no excuse for not putting yourself in your customers' shoes and experiencing your products and services the way they do.

Just being present with your customers is a good way to do this. In addition to shopping incognito, I like to ease into the background and simply watch and listen to what goes on in our stores. I'm like a lab student observing an experiment through a two-way mirror. Even at our World Bearquarters in Saint Louis, I frequently walk around the office. By doing so, I get to eavesdrop on the conversations our associates are having about concerns expressed by our Guests. It's yet another way I put myself in our Guests' shoes.

Figure out ways you can blend into the background of your company, so you can observe customer interactions without influencing them. If you run a clothing boutique, for example, spend time on the sales floor and carefully observe your customers as they shop. Do they have trouble navigating down the aisles? Have you hung clothing for a petite-sized woman on the highest racks? Does everyone have to ask for directions to the dressing room? Are customers overlooking the accessories?

If you manage a professional office in a high-rise building, take a minute to linger in the lobby, instead of dashing upstairs to your desk. How do the security guards and the receptionist interact with visitors? Does anyone get lost on his or her way to the elevator? Is the building directory easy to read? Do people have a place to wipe their feet and shake the rain off their umbrellas? Or perhaps even plastic sleeves to cover those wet umbrellas?

> *Ease into the background and simply watch and listen to what's going on.*

Some businesses hire secret shoppers. These people can provide some valuable insights. (Build-A-Bear Workshop doesn't use secret shoppers; I prefer to query our real Guests about what they think of the business.)

If you hire secret shoppers, be mindful that you measure those things that really matter most to your customers. And very carefully select your secret shoppers. If you plan to base changes and policies on their opinions, make sure you understand their frame of reference—the places they shop every day and are comparing you against. For the most part, I think you ought to solicit the opinions of your real customers, instead of paid observers. They are, after all, your customers every single day and the feedback you glean from them is the more valuable than what you'll get from hired hands.

We're all customers of someone every day of our lives. Draw on these experiences, good and bad, for guidance on how to treat your own customers.

I recently picked up a bottle of vitamins formulated specifically for women over 50. The product usage and warning information was squeezed onto the back of the bottle in the finest print I'd ever seen. It was so tiny, I couldn't read it. Obviously, that manufacturer hadn't taken the time to see the product through the customer's eyes. If they had, they would have realized that their target customers—women over 50 like me—couldn't see the information at all. That's just plain dumb!

Find ways to observe customer interactions without influencing them.

I'm not alone in my belief that to be successful you've got to experience your product or service as a customer does.

Southwest Airlines requires its executives to fly the airline on a regular basis. They travel anonymously to ensure they're treated no differently from other passengers. At the same time, they sit beside regular customers at the airport and on the plane to find out what they like and don't like about Southwest. That's the ultimate focus group.

Volvo Trucks North America also goes to great lengths to see itself through its customers' eyes. The company designs and manufactures cabs for tractor trailers. Engineers who work there have the option of earning their own truck driver's license. This is an excellent idea because when these engineers learn how to drive a truck, they also get a better understanding of how to design it better. Once they've had the experience of sitting in the driver's seat of a big rig, they have a much better perspective on where the controls should be placed and why. They're then able to design the vehicle with the driver's safety and comfort in mind. Simply put, once these engineers drive a few miles in the customer's seat, they perform much better at their own jobs.

Solicit the opinions of real customers, instead of hiring paid observers.

You'll become better at your job and your business will operate more smoothly if you take the same approach as well.

Learn from Your Customers

As you should have gathered from the previous chapter, your customers are your best source of market research. They can provide the answers to all your questions about what will and won't sell. They're also your best inspiration for new products. You're crazy not to tap into this valuable resource and put what you learn to use for your business. Customers are the energy behind your brand.

Current customers are your number-one source of potential new products.

Many business owners don't take the time to learn from their customers until they have some pending project that must be completed or a crisis that needs to be addressed. That's the time when they might send out surveys, hold focus groups, or start digging through old correspondence, searching for clues on how consumers behave.

In my mind, this is the wrong way to go about it. Learning from your customers should be an everyday occurrence.

One of the best ways is to take a snapshot of everyone who buys from you or inquires about your products or services. When I say snapshot, I don't mean it in the literal sense. I'm talking about compiling a dossier, if you will, on every customer. The information included in that file will vary depending on your type of business. We have quite a sophisticated customer database comprised of information collected when Guests name their bears in our stores or sign up for our online mailing list. (We use this information only internally and do not share it with any outside parties.) We also have a separate Guest feedback database, including their letters. We routinely mine the database to answer questions like who's shopping at our stores, what are our best-selling items, where have people suggested that we build stores, and which markets without a current location have the highest concentration of Build-A-Bear Workshop customers. In those ways, it's an amazing strategic tool.

Our database contains thousands of records and is very broad in scope. Yet, we can answer complex questions very quickly because it's all computerized. I know many people are still uncomfortable with computers and technology. I'm often surprised by how primitively some people operate their businesses and how they still do tasks the complicated, old-fashioned way because their systems aren't computerized. If that describes you, it's time to get over it. In today's world, you need automated processes and access to e-mail if you want to keep up with the competition. If you don't have the necessary computer skills, learn them or hire someone who does.

> *Compile a dossier on everyone who buys from you. This is your best source of market research.*

If we had to go through every record by hand, our database wouldn't be nearly as useful as it is. We'd waste time analyzing data—time that could be better spent addressing Guests' needs. I suppose there are some businesses that could get by keeping handwritten files on their customers. I know several hairdressers who use spiral notebooks to keep track of what services they've performed for which clients. That way when the client comes in for her next cut or color, the stylist can see at a glance what she requested last time. Even in that example, computerizing the records would make them more useful. The stylist could punch a few keys on a computer to see which clients are due for haircuts and send them a friendly reminder in the mail. The stylist could also keep better track of inventory and use this information when reordering hair coloring or permanent solution from suppliers.

An upscale restaurant might keep notes about its regular customers, indicating their dining preferences. Water, no lemon. Likes a particular waiter. Always orders the steak rare and will send it back if it's overcooked. The low-tech way to do this would be in an alphabetized index-card file. But those cards could easily be misplaced or, on a busy night, the maître d' might forget to pull a customer's card. If the records were instead computerized and integrated with the reservation system, those preferences would be noted when the customer reserved a table.

> *In today's world, you need automated processes if you want to keep up with the competition.*

One of my favorite hotels, Wyndham, uses a very similar system. Guests have the option of signing up for the Wyndham ByRequest program. It's the company's version of a preferred customer program. When you join, you pick your favorite perks, and whenever you check in to any Wyndham property you'll find your selections waiting for you. I always have bottled water, extra hand towels, and feather pillows delivered to my room. You can also specify your preference for a smoking or nonsmoking room, extra towels, down pillows, and other amenities. Wyndham has successfully created a mechanism for learning about its customers while also pleasing them—and it makes frequent travelers more likely to seek out a Wyndham while on the road.

In addition to building a database, there are plenty of other ways you can learn from your customers—both actively through contests, questionnaires, surveys, focus groups, and conversations, and passively through observation.

I like to venture into my customers' world to see how they live their lives, like a safari lover who travels to remote places to observe animals in their natural environments.

Long before starting Build-A-Bear Workshop, when I'd go pick up Katie and her brother Jack from school, I'd make note of what shoes the kids were wearing and take that information back to my colleagues at May. It's the same thing that fashion designers do when they stroll the streets of Paris and other places where trendsetters hang out, looking for inspiration. I still like going to schools (especially on the first day of a new school year) to see how kids dress and play, while at the same time figuring out how we can apply those trends to teddy bears. I shop in the same stores where they shop—Limited Too, The Children's Place, and Disney—and hang out at places where real people hang out—soccer games, movie theaters, fast-food restaurants, and amusement parks. These settings are great learning laboratories for me because they happen to be places overrun with our core demographic. Your clientele might mingle elsewhere, say at trade shows, late-night watering holes, spas, symposiums, the symphony, or the local cafeteria restaurant. You need to be where they are on a regular basis, and pay attention to how they behave.

> *Other ways to learn about your customers include contests, questionnaires, surveys, focus groups, conversations, and observation.*

Of course, you must also observe and engage your customers at your place of business and act on the lessons you learn. During our initial months in business, we closely watched how Guests shopped in our stores. We very quickly determined that a 2,000-square-foot footprint was too small to accommodate customer flow and could easily become overcrowded. We also observed that lines backed up at cash registers and that everyone—and I do mean everyone—wanted to give their stuffed animals a name. We followed those lessons as we built additional stores. We made the newer locations bigger and added more cash registers and kiosks at the Name Me station.

When learning from your customers, remember to dig deeper than just determining what they're buying. You should also figure out *why*.

Why has always been a big word for me. As a kid, I think I probably drove my parents crazy with my curiosity. My constant refrain was "Why?" It still amazes me that a single word can provide enlightenment to a curious child. In business, asking why opens a world of possibilities and delivers numerous insights.

Find out where your customers live and where they like to go.

People often cannot cogently explain their motivations. How many times has your "Why?" been answered with a noncommittal, "Oh, I don't know. Just because." In journalism school, I learned how to ask the same question in many different ways until I finally got the answer. I use those same interview techniques when talking with Guests and trying to learn more about them and their relationship to our company. This is really not that hard to do. In fact, it comes down to simple conversational skills. Actively listen to what the other person is saying and respond with more specific questions.

What do you like to do?
Why do you like it?

Where else have you been today?

Why did you come?

Where else could you have gone?

Why didn't you go there?

What don't you like?

Why?

Is there anything you'd like to see more of?

Will you come here again?

Will you bring your friends?

What would make you come here?

What can I do to make your day better?

What can I do to make you smile?

Always ask the key question: why?

Imagine the wealth of information you would get if you asked just one client these questions. Multiply that by the whole universe of people who do business with you and it should be clear just how much you can learn about being successful in business directly from those who matter most—your customers.

Build an Advisory Board

I f you want to make your customers happy, talk to them and listen to what they have to say. It's a simple premise, but many businesses discount the importance of having direct and frequent conversations with those who pay their bills.

> *If you want to make your customers happy, listen to what they have to say.*

As you already know, I spend a large amount of my time interacting with Guests in our stores and talking to them about their preferences. At Build-A-Bear Workshop, we also have a formal mechanism for collecting feedback from children (our primary demographic).

Starting way back with Katie and her brother, Jack, I created an advisory board of children I could call upon for advice and feedback on our products. I was excited to learn everything I could to make this business better for them. This group was dubbed our Cub Advisory Board. It still exists today, and we seek their input often. Kids were, and continue to be, an important source of ideas for my business—and for me. I trust their opinions.

Our core advisory board is comprised of children ages 6 through 18. They are mostly kids from the Saint Louis area. Some are children of my friends and associates, making it easier to call them in for meetings and focus groups at our World Bearquarters. As our company has expanded, however, we've selected kids from around the country to be advisers. Even if they can't come to Missouri for meetings, I solicit their feedback and advice through e-mail. There's one particular group of children who e-mail me a lot—some members send a note every day. I call them my Focus Group Gang. Whenever I need kiddie insights, I send out a note asking them for help (with their parents' permission of course). For example, I might write, "We're looking to make Build-A-Bear Workshop parties better. How can we do that?"

I really listen to what my young advisers have to say because they've never steered me wrong. If they don't like an idea, we won't proceed with it. We heed their advice, particularly as it relates to merchandising. After all, they represent the demographic that is buying our products. We listen to what they have to say about which animals to carry, what those furry characters should look like, what clothing and accessories we should sell, and where we should build new stores.

Create an advisory board comprised of members of your core audience who can be called upon regularly for feedback and advice.

I remember once showing the Cub Advisory Board members our Floppy Kitty. Originally, the cat was a vibrant yellowy-orange, a hue that one cub adviser described as "like macaroni and cheese."

"That's great," I remember saying. "Everybody likes macaroni and cheese, right?"

"Yeah," piped up the little girl. "But you wouldn't eat your cat."

My adult mind didn't make that childlike—yet important—connection. Based on that conversation, we changed the color of Floppy Kitty, toning down the brightness.

For any business that wants to stay in touch with its customers, it's imperative to have an advisory board. In fact, if you are in the start-up phase of your business, make this a priority. If you start seeking customer input early, you will be able to tailor your business to their specific and unique needs.

There are companies that specialize in customer feedback panels, though we rarely retain that kind of help and I don't believe it's necessary. If you keep a record of the customer feedback you receive or pay attention to those faces you see over and over again, you'll be able to organize your own advisory board. (This will save a lot of money as well.)

> *If you seek customer input early, you'll be able to tailor your business to their specific and unique needs.*

We built our Cub Advisory Board using existing Guests—kids who were already shopping and spending money with us. We had no difficulty identifying or recruiting them for board membership. Additionally, I save every e-mail and letter I receive from Guests, making it easy to identify those who are the most active and loyal.

Using this information, we've been able to create a vocal and effective Guest advisory board. We did make one mistake when setting up the board. When we recruited kids, we didn't set a limit on their length of service or identify at what age they would have to retire. Once they're a part of our board, nobody wants to leave! As a result, we have numerous advisers emeritus—high school and college students outside of our core demographic—who still like to offer their two cents' worth about the business. (As our founding Cub Advisory Board members have grown up, we've recruited other younger kids to serve. But the board ranks are much larger than the 20 or so kids we originally intended.)

To ensure that your customer advisory board stays fresh, relevant, and relatively small, I suggest creating membership rules. You could allow members to serve until they reach a certain age (an excellent idea if your business targets a younger demographic, as Build-A-Bear Workshop does). Or, you could have members serve set two-year or four-year terms, like elected officials do. If you choose this approach, remember to stagger the terms so there are always new and old members on the board.

> *Save every e-mail and letter you get from customers.*

Solicit the help of your customer advisory board frequently, but not so much that it becomes unmanageable for you and/or your staff, and not so often that you become a nuisance to your customers. Ideally we try to hold at least semiannual meetings of the Cub Advisory Board, and I think that's a good frequency. Advisory board members are willing to attend occasional meetings. But, like all of us, they're pretty busy and don't have time for a regimented meeting schedule.

> *To keep your advisory board fresh, stagger the terms and set specific limits on how long someone can be a part of it.*

I use e-mail to keep in touch with our board members in the interim. If I need quick help on a project, I'll shoot the cubs or Focus Group Gang a message. I've found they're always willing to help. E-mail is less intrusive than a meeting or even a telephone call. Or we might bring in a subset of our Cub Advisory Board for a quick review.

One of the big questions most people have about customer advisory boards is whether you should pay people to serve. I don't think it's a good idea to write checks for customer feedback. Above all, you want customer advisory board members to be honest. If they're on your payroll, these customers may not feel comfortable offering criticism or negative opinions. Dr. Tony Carter, a professor of sales and marketing management and author of *Customer Advisory Boards* (Best Business Books: Haworth Press, 2003), is of the same mind. "Customer advisory boards can, and probably should, operate without paying fees to the members," he writes. "Besides being cost-effective, this makes sure that people never start saying what they think management wants to hear."

While it's not a good idea to compensate advisory board members for service, it's perfectly acceptable to thank them for their service with occasional discounts, gift certificates, and gifts. If you discover that someone is interested in how they'll be rewarded, you might not want that person on your advisory board. Our Cub Advisors don't serve on the board because they want compensation. For them, it's about being listened to and seeing their ideas in motion. We try to be a role model for these children and provide a place where they can make a contribution. They're assisting me with my company, and I hope I'm helping them learn about business in the process.

When I was in high school, I had the chance to serve on the teen board at my local department store. I have never forgotten that experience. It was a major reason I considered retail as a career in the first place. I hope that our Cub Advisory Board members learn as much from this opportunity as I did back then. This seems to be the case. One Cub Advisor told me he eventually wants to be president of Build-A-Bear Workshop. That made my day, and I hope that wish comes true.

> *It's not a good idea to pay people to be on your advisory board, though you can reward them in other ways for their service.*

An advisory board is a relatively inexpensive way to connect with your customers. American businesses spend billions of dollars every year hiring research firms to study consumer behavior. You can accomplish much the same result, for a fraction of the cost, by convening a meeting of your best customers and asking for their opinions.

There's no reason not to have a customer advisory board. You'll discover ways to improve the products and services you sell. You'll engender customer loyalty and perhaps discover a few brand evangelists. And you're likely to see an improvement in your sales and profits when you take the time to listen.

Bring Out the Child in Everyone

Someone once said that my inner child never quite grew up. After all, my life revolves around teddy bears, and I spend my days talking to little kids. I guess that does make me somewhat of an expert on childlike behavior. But the truth is, I'm a big believer that even the oldest among us can appreciate a little playfulness every now and then. We all crave fun, and isn't that what being a kid is all about?

We all crave fun.

When you run a business like mine, it's easy to create the kind of atmosphere where every Guest, regardless of age, can act like a kid and feel comfortable doing it. We offer the same interactive experience to our Guests, whether they're 3 or 103, and it's their choice how far they take it and how involved they become. We have some adults who are very reserved as they make their bears. There are others who just overflow with enthusiasm and go through each station with gusto. They give their hearts a big smooch, jump up and down, and sing silly songs with their friends. They preen over their newly made bears and try several outfits before deciding on just the right one. They cuddle their animals, name them, and enthusiastically accept the free stickers and ribbons we give away. And they walk out with huge grins on their faces. (If you ask me, these adults have the best mind-set of all, and they're probably going to live longer because they let themselves have fun.)

> *Being a kid means having few responsibilities, not needing to worry about things, and knowing you are taken care of. Those are the same things your customers want.*

I know some of you more "mature" readers are ready to close the book now or flip ahead to the next chapter. "I run a serious business that caters to adults, not kids," you say. "What lessons could I possibly learn from you here?" The answer is, plenty!

Think about what it really means to be a kid. Having fun is certainly a part of it. But being a kid also means having few responsibilities, not needing to worry about things, and knowing someone else is around to take care of you. Aren't those the same traits that customers demand of the companies they frequent?

You should make it as easy and pleasant as possible for people to do business with you. You're taking care of them, not the other way around. You're handling all the hassles, so they don't have to worry about anything.

Again, I think this is pretty commonsense advice, but experience has shown that not everyone follows this principle. For example, have you ever custom-ordered furniture? With all the assembly work that goes on overseas, some manufacturers are notoriously slow in completing orders. I think it ought to be the job of the store that sells this furniture to monitor any manufacturing delays and report those to the consumer. What usually happens is that after 12 or more weeks of waiting, the customer calls the store and asks, "Where's my furniture?" The answer is usually "I don't know" or something equally uninformative. The customer has been left to worry for three months that the furniture isn't coming and has been forced to take responsibility for monitoring that order, a job that clearly belongs to the store.

> *Make it as easy and pleasant as possible for people to do business with you.*

What about contractors who don't line up the correct permits, inspections, and licenses until their client asks about them? Or the waitress who never bothers to refill a diner's drink glass? Or the computer software programmer who leaves the network vulnerable to viruses and attacks from hackers? They're not taking care of their customers, and in some cases, are instead creating some serious problems.

Given these examples, wouldn't you rather be treated like a kid in your business dealings? And wouldn't you prefer to treat your customers that way?

Here's some advice on how to make doing business with your company fun, even if your customers are adults and your product is more serious than teddy bears.

Give Away Stuff

This tried-and-true approach has been used by everybody from cell phone companies (free nights and weekend minutes) to cosmetics companies (free gift with purchase) to airlines (free flights with your frequent-flier miles). My dad, who was a lighting salesman before he retired, used to travel around with his car and briefcase packed full of samples and small gifts he'd give away to everyone he called on. Even small gifts make people happy.

> *Customers of all ages like free stuff, to be pampered, and to feel like their whole family is welcome.*

Pamper Your Customers

Whenever I get a cold, I remember how much different it was to be sick as a child. My mom was there to chase the aches and pains away with her kisses and attentiveness. Being sick always went hand in hand with getting pampered. If you weren't feeling well, you'd always be showered with all your favorite foods, TV shows, toys, and stuffed animals. I certainly haven't outgrown my fondness for being pampered, and I think many people share that feeling. You don't have to manage a spa to be in the pampering business.

Welcome Their Families

There's a lot to be gained from making your business family friendly, even if you're not selling a family-oriented product or service. For instance, I'm always surprised when I go to car dealerships and see how adult-oriented they are. But visit any car lot, and you'll see a lot of people roaming around with their kids, who are usually whining because they're bored. As a result, the parents usually cut their shopping trip short. I've never understood why more dealerships don't give kids something to do while their parents are looking at cars. They could show cartoons in the lobby; they could give away Matchbox car replicas to youngsters, or, better yet, have kid-sized versions of the vehicles so the children can experience the product for themselves and have a say in the buying decision. Any of these items would further occupy the kids, giving their parents more time to shop, and the salespeople more time to close the deal. I can't think of many businesses that wouldn't benefit from being more family friendly.

> *On occasion, allow yourself to think and act like a kid, regardless of how old you are.*

By the way, one day the children who played in your showroom and felt valued will be back to buy their own real car. They are more likely to remember your showroom and brand as their first place of choice. And when they do make that first car purchase, be it new or used, let it be a celebration! Even if the parents are handing down their old car, offer a special Sweet 16 free tune-up to the family. Aren't they then sure to buy their replacement car from you? The opportunities to wow your customers with childlike surprises and celebrations are endless.

I hope you see now that treating customers like kids isn't a bad thing, and I trust that you'll find clever ways to integrate all these strategies into your own business. I also encourage you to allow yourself to think and act like a child on occasion as well. I know that my most successful moments in business have been when I could do just that. They've been my most enjoyable, too.

Spending More Creates More Value

I tend to think of the money we spend on our business not as an expense, but as an investment.

In life, we're constantly presented with the choice between spending and scrimping. Sometimes scrimping is the right answer. What difference does it really make if you buy generic versus brand-name paper towels? But for some things, spending is by far the best option. Is paying tuition at an Ivy League school a splurge or an investment in the future? Is it a waste of money to spend $50,000 remodeling your kitchen if the face-lift raises the value of the house by $75,000? And when buying a car, isn't it wise to spend a few thousand more on a model with more airbags and other safety features?

Think carefully about the long-term consequences of your spending.

When faced with expenditures in your business, think carefully about the long-term consequences of your spending. Weigh the future impact of that investment against the near-term challenges that will be created if you part with the money. Then, make the all-important choice: spend or scrimp.

Money spent wisely now will pay off for you in the future.

> *Money spent wisely now will pay off for you in the future.*

I can list of string of costly investments I made when the business was young, knowing that these expenditures would provide a sturdy foundation for the future. For instance, we hired experts to translate my ideas into a brand. We invested heavily in our web site, creating both a community and an online marketplace. We spent more than most companies would have designing our bears and making sure our fashions and accessories were as realistic and soft and huggable as possible.

> *You can never go wrong spending money on customer goodwill.*

These expenditures were worthwhile and have paid off in spades. They helped Build-A-Bear Workshop become a brand, not just a retailer. They enabled us to function efficiently as we've grown. And they raised our value proposition among consumers.

Beyond my own examples, I can think of many instances when spending in the present would create more value for your company in the future. Placing advertisements that position your company as *the* source for a particular product or service, buying equipment that automates time-consuming tasks and streamlines your operation, and cross-training your employees to do various jobs all fall into this category.

In addition, I don't think you can ever go wrong spending money on customer goodwill. We have a separate budget for Guest surprises, those little things we do to show our customers how much we appreciate them. These surprises include gift cards, promotional items like free calendars, and stickers and merchandise giveaways, such as backpacks, key chains, and other accessories.

Every year, we spend quite a bit on promotional expenses like these, but I don't feel it's money wasted. Nothing appeals to consumers more than a free gift. When we send out $5 gift certificates, most Guests who come in to redeem them spend far more than that. Sometimes when we give away free accessories, we make the gift conditional on a purchase. Even when we don't, we always more than make our money back.

> *You always win when customers smile.*

When you spend (or should I say *invest?*) money on customer goodwill or give away something at no charge—whether it is a free gift, free shipping, or free gift wrapping—you're raising the perceived value of your products. You always win when customers smile.

Some industries, like the cosmetics business, have done this for ages. Who among us really needs those small sample sizes in those adorable bags? We want the bags! And we often buy the cheapest qualifying item they sell. If you're a woman, you're no doubt smiling because you know how often you are attracted to this technique. It's not a sale, but a gift with purchase (GWP). I have even seen customers stop at cosmetics counters asking for the date of the next GWP.

Remember to view your business expenditures, both big and small, as investments in your future success. Always be prudent in your spending, but don't let frugality hamstring you. Spend when doing so will create more value within your company.

This is our first Build-A-Bear Workshop store. It opened in October 1997 at the Saint Louis Galleria. We still adhere to the same basic look and floor plan at all of our stores around the world.

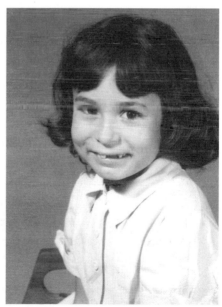

This is me at age seven, about the time my own teddy bear taught me how important furry best friends can be to people of all ages. This little girl is living proof of how "lucky" you can get when you work really hard. Even back then, I believed in finding your passion and going for it!

This is Katie Burkhardt, my good friend and the inspiration for starting Build-A-Bear Workshop. She's standing next to our company mascot, Bearemy, at the opening of our store in Japan.

Kids aren't afraid to speak their minds, and they have amazing things to say. They also represent our primary customer demographic. That's why our Cub Advisory Board, pictured here, is so important. They all got together in person for the signing of our first international franchisee agreement.

This picture captures the relaxed atmosphere and excitement our associates feel each morning before opening the doors to Build-A-Bear Workshop Guests. When you embrace a relaxed atmosphere, both your employees and your customers are bound to have fun!

Never underestimate the power of using your existing customers to build buzz. As you can see from this photo, taken at one of our Los Angeles, California, stores, oftentimes loyal Guests bring lots of friends with them, who then frequently become loyal customers themselves.

This is the front of our New York City store, located at Fifth Avenue and 46th Street. It's the biggest Build-A-Bear Workshop store to date anywhere in the world. Although we were excited about opening this location, we didn't do it right away. We took on this large-scale project only when the brand was financially, operationally, and emotionally ready.

Chelsey, pictured here with me and her grandmother, is one of our loyal Guests in Nova Scotia. She visits the store frequently looking for the latest product introductions. Introducing new items and services gives your customers a reason to come back and see you again and again.

In this photo, I'm proud to be surrounded by our Huggable Heroes—kids we've recognized from around the country who are making a difference in their communities. I firmly believe that, regardless of what business you're in, it's up to you to make the world a better place for all of us to live in.

We cultivate customer evangelists through our party program. When Guests have fun at a party, they want to come back and make more new friends.

Our signature Cub Condo carrying case is more than just a shopping bag. It also serves as a walking billboard for our brand. It's yet another reminder of the importance of thinking outside of the box (or, in this case, the bag).

There is really no limit to how and where you can market your business. In fact, we created a store on wheels—the Build-A-Bear Workshop On Tour—that takes the experience brought by our company beyond the malls and into all sorts of places where families can go to have a lot of fun.

A teddy bear hug is understood in any language. Here is The Bear Promise sign in our Denmark store. Kids all over the world recite this promise in many languages, but they are all pledging to do the same thing: be their new friend's number-one pal.

To be successful in whatever you do, you've got to put your heart into it. As depicted in this photo, each Guest has a chance to put a heart sealed with love inside their furry friends. This is a signature concept developed by our company.

Here I am with Hannah, the winner of our Furbulous Fashion Design contest, and her family. They all came to New York City to see her winning outfit debut on our Macy's Thanksgiving Day Parade float. Creating fun and unique events keeps customers engaged in your brand.

Don't Cater to All Audiences

Growth can be a tricky thing. Once you get a taste of success, it's natural to crave more. Whether your company is public or private, you may feel pressure from outside investors— or yourself—to bring in more business to boost revenues.

Sometimes, it seems that the easiest way to do this is by attracting new and different customers and broadening your focus beyond your core user. That's a disastrous way to grow.

No matter the outside pressures nor how tempting success is, you must stay focused on serving your core customer group. Don't fall into the trap that so many businesses do of thinking they can serve everybody well. Lose focus, and you'll lose customers.

> *Attracting different customers and broadening your focus beyond your core user is a disastrous way to grow.*

It may be true that you can sell your products outside your core user segment. But be careful not to take your eye off the ball and divert resources (financial and otherwise) beyond this primary core audience.

Despite our varied customer base at Build-A-Bear Workshop, we resist the urge to move outside our core user for two primary reasons. First, there are too many other competitors—most of them indirect like clothing stores, video game arcades, and toy stores—that also cater to these same Guest segments. Second, if we stop focusing on our core audience, there's a good chance we'll lose their business altogether to those indirect competitors that offer alternative fun, interactive experiences.

And when you lose customers, it's very hard to get them back.

A myriad of factors can cause companies to divert their focus and lose sight of their core audience. These include changing trends, the economy, investor pressure for more revenue, successful competitors, and newcomers within the business who don't understand the target market. Always listen to your customers first and the marketplace second.

Many businesses have buckled to external pressures, and they've suffered financially as a result.

FAO Schwarz was once revered as the greatest toy store ever, and the place every child dreamed of visiting. But the company tried to get too big, and in doing so, lost sight of its uniqueness. FAO Schwarz opened too many stores in mediocre markets, a fact that contributed to its Chapter 11 bankruptcy in 2003. The company made a number of mistakes, but one of its biggest was abandoning its core customers. That move undermined FAO Schwarz's 100-year-old reputation as an exclusive store where you could find expensive and hard-to-get toys from around the world.

No matter what the temptations or outside pressures, stay focused on your primary customer group.

Here's another example from the toy industry. About six years ago, executives at Toys "R" Us decided to streamline the business by reducing the number of items carried in stores. I'm sure there was a sound financial reason for doing this, but the action backfired. Assortment was a key differentiator for the company. Toys "R" Us carried a great deal of merchandise that couldn't be bought anywhere else. That was a fantastic attraction for parents looking to buy their kids something new and different. With the reduced product offerings, Toys "R" Us became no different than Wal-Mart, which easily won market share with its low prices.

Hot Topic, which specializes in selling music-related fashion, is a company that persists in serving its core audience despite outside pressures to do otherwise. Orv Madden started the business in 1988, realizing there was a large market of teenagers and young adults interested in buying clothing inspired by their favorite bands. Many of Hot Topic's clothes have a "goth" look, and they're targeted to fans of rock, punk rock, and alternative groups.

Right now, such clothing doesn't appeal to mainstream teen buyers, who prefer the preppy looks being marketed by other retailers like Abercrombie & Fitch and American Eagle Outfitters. This fact has negatively impacted Hot Topic's same-store sales. But the retailer is not abandoning its core customer or changing its product assortment to take advantage of the preppy trend. On its web site, the company says, "Music is where Hot Topic began, and it firmly remains at the core of everything Hot Topic does." That's an admirable position— and I think the right one for the company. Fashions change, and Hot Topic must keep up with new trends, but only as they relate to its core audience.

Dunkin' Donuts has also stayed true to its core audience, despite outside pressures. When Krispy Kreme Doughnuts began making headlines and generating hype in the late 1990s, Dunkin' Donuts didn't change the basics of how it did business. It added some new types of doughnuts, but didn't try to compete on Krispy Kreme's brand promise of "hot doughnuts now."

> *Always listen to your customers first and the marketplace second.*

The company kept serving and paying attention to the needs of the millions of customers worldwide who make Dunkin' Donuts part of their daily ritual. For these customers, it's the coffee—and not just the doughnuts—that is most important. Dunkin' Donuts serves more than one billion cups of coffee every year, making it America's largest retailer of coffee by the cup. Although its lattes and Dunkaccinos may appeal to Starbucks' customers, Dunkin' Donuts still mainly caters to those who prefer a more traditional cup of coffee, using a 55-year-old recipe for its brew.

One of the biggest challenges any marketer faces is identifying and then staying focused on its core users despite outside market forces. The demands and needs of your primary audience will surely change. To keep their business, you've got to grow with them. But be careful how you read that statement.

Though I still love and respect the insights of my good friend Katie, at 20 she is no longer our core customer. We didn't change Build-A-Bear Workshop to suit her needs as she experienced adolescence, navigated high school, or entered college. We stayed focused on the 10-year-old little girl who helped bring this company to market and who has fueled its success for the past eight years.

> *The demands and needs of your primary audience will surely change. You've got to keep up with them.*

A whole other group of 10-year-old girls has taken on the role of core Guest for us. We are changing as a company every day, tailoring our products, services, and experiences to today's Katies and their ever-changing tastes in fashion and trends.

Staying focused on your core customer must be your primary mission in business. That doesn't mean you can never do things to cultivate other audiences. But you must be certain that your quest to gain new customers doesn't alienate your loyal base.

Until recently, we spent nearly 95 percent of our advertising dollars on the retention of existing Guests. We would send them mailings, coupons, and gift cards to encourage them to return to our stores.

In 2003, we decided we needed to change that strategy and instead use more money to attract *new* Guests to the stores. Now, 75 percent of our advertising budget is earmarked for new Guest acquisition. That wasn't a change we made lightly. We tested the new advertising initiative in eight markets before rolling it out nationally to ensure we weren't alienating our existing audience.

We found that these refocused ads brought in *both* new and existing Guests. That's because we wisely stayed focused on our core audience and aimed our national advertising at them—not at a wide group that had little interest in our products. We changed how we spent our advertising dollars, but not whom we spent it on.

The old saying that you can't be all things to all people is particularly true if you want to deliver an excellent product with an exceptional experience. Cater to your core customer, instead of trying to reach everyone you possibly can. That's how you'll most effectively gain the maximum amount of traction.

Ensure That Each Person Feels Special

On paper, I've been in the clothing, shoe, and teddy bear making businesses. Someone who doesn't understand how I think and operate would say, "She sells a whole bunch of stuff." But I'd argue that I'm really in the *relationship* business. I fill an emotional niche with special products that mean something to the people who buy them.

My primary job—indeed the job of everyone at Build-A-Bear Workshop—is to make my Guests feel special. I believe that's why we should all be in business, no matter what our profession. Profits are important, but success is measured in more than dollars and cents. Whether you're working for yourself or someone else, you ought to do everything in your power to make your customers and the people you work alongside feel special.

Your primary job is to make your customers feel special.

I believe we each have a moral imperative to behave this way. It's the way I live my life—and I can tell you from experience that following it pays off in so many ways—both personal and financial. That's yet another reason to do everything in your power to make others feel special. You might make it without doing this, but you won't be as successful as you could be. This has truly been my experience many times over.

I know it's easier to think of your company in terms of what you sell, and sometimes it is hard to connect that end product to the people who are consuming it. After all, not every item is as cuddly as a teddy bear. Yet, with every product, there is an opportunity to connect emotionally with your customer. Maybe it's through the sales pitch or the safety features that competitors don't offer. Perhaps it's through pricing.

> *Taking care of your customers will lead to many personal and financial rewards.*

This connection is what makes a person buy a particular product and service. Most spending is emotional, even for the most basic and mundane goods and services. There's a reason I bought my refrigerator from a particular appliance store. There's a reason my husband takes our cars to the same mechanic every time they need service or repairs. There's a reason my coauthor, Amy Joyner, drives an hour each way to get her teeth cleaned by the same dentist she visited as a kid. There's something about the product, the place, or the people who work there that makes us want to do business with them. And no matter the reason—price, selection, honesty, or convenience—emotion dictates why each is our preferred place of business.

I'm sure you've interviewed a job candidate who described himself as a "people person." It's hard not to roll your eyes when you hear someone say that. But that's what we all should strive to be. And every business should be a "people company."

The pharmaceutical industry? It's about people who need the company's drugs to stay healthy and alive. The furniture industry? It's about people who want to furnish their homes with things they love and that will comfort them. The oil industry? It's about people who buy gas to fill up their cars, heating oil for winter, and petroleum-derived plastic products for everyday use and convenience.

> *If you give people a reason to do business with you, they will travel far and wide to do so.*

It doesn't take much to make someone feel special, especially in a buyer-seller relationship. The required ingredients are: quality products; attentive, undivided service; personalized communications, such as correspondence that is addressed to a specific recipient; salespeople who remember the names of their customers; special privileges, such as Chico's Passport Club and White House | Black Market's Black Book Club, both of which are loyalty programs that give customers a discount once they've spent a certain amount with the company; involving the customer in product decisions, whether by offering the option to customize an item or soliciting their feedback through surveys and other similar mechanisms; being available, as I am, to answer customer letters; and just having a phone number or place on the Web where customers can go with questions about purchases or their account.

My nursery school teacher, Mrs. Fisher, taught me just how easy it is to make someone feel special. When I was growing up, kids didn't go to kindergarten at public school. But nursery schools like mine offered the equivalent for kids who were a year shy of first grade. Even from the early age of 4, I liked school and had a real aptitude for it. I was doing so well that my mom asked the nursery school if I could enroll in the school's kindergarten program a year early to get a jump start. Mrs. Fisher agreed to let me enroll, with the understanding that I'd have to repeat the class the following year.

Among the required ingredients to make people feel special: quality products, attentive service, personalized communications, and involving them in product decisions.

I was younger and smaller than the rest of the kids, but Mrs. Fisher never singled me out in a negative way. She always made me feel special with her demeanor and her attitude toward me. When all the older kindergartners graduated to first grade, I didn't feel left out as the only one not receiving my diploma. She asked me to be her special assistant on graduation day and made me feel special because I got to live my wonderful kindergarten year all over again.

I guess it is true that we learn our most important lessons in kindergarten. Follow Mrs. Fisher's example and make the people you deal with on a daily basis feel special because of the way you treat them. A little kindness goes a long way.

Answer Customer Letters

Want to know how to make your customers *really* mad? Ignore them.

I can already hear you rumbling, "What kind of fool would ignore his or her customers? I never would. I'm not that rude. I listen to what they have to stay. I respond to their requests and concerns."

> By ignoring those customers who write to you, you're missing an opportunity to create free goodwill, cultivate loyalty, collect valuable feedback, and connect with them.

Maybe so when that customer is standing right in front of you, or when they're on the other end of the telephone. But what happens when customers write to you? Do you answer their letters or reply to their e-mail messages? If not, you should. By ignoring your customers in this way, you're missing the opportunity to create free goodwill, cultivate loyalty, and collect valuable feedback.

I invite all of our Guests (and associates as well) to write or e-mail me, and store managers often pass along Guest correspondence. I personally reply to every letter and e-mail message I receive.

I'm not aware of many other CEOs who do that, and I really don't understand why. It's not that hard to respond to a Guest or answer their request. With e-mail, it's even easier.

> *Everyone who writes to you is a current or potential customer.*

Everybody who writes to me is a current or potential Guest. I want to treat them as well as possible and attend to their needs, just as I would in person at one of our stores. If a child or an adult has taken the time to write to me with praise, a question, a suggestion, or a complaint, I owe them the courtesy of a response. This isn't a job I can hand off to an assistant or some other department. The customer wrote to *me*; the reply should come from *me*.

I probably spend several hours a day reading and responding to Guest letters and e-mails. Some I skim and respond to very quickly; others I file so I can spend more time reading them and crafting a response.

> *If someone takes the time to send you a note, you owe that person the courtesy of a response.*

It's really not that difficult to answer your customers' letters. There are things I do to simplify the task and save time, which you can easily replicate in your own business.

The best time-saving advice is to use technology to your advantage. I've tried to direct Guests to correspond with me electronically, via e-mail, because that's the easiest way for them to get in touch. In turn, I can provide a quick response.

> *The best time-saving advice is to use technology to your advantage.*

Here are some other tricks I use to speed and simplify my correspondence with customers.

- *Create standardized responses.* A lot of Guests ask me the same questions. When are you going to build a store in my area? How can I get a job at Build-A-Bear Workshop? Do you sell franchises? I have standardized replies for each of those questions.
- *Personalize every letter.* Even when using a standard reply, I take the time to write a personalized greeting. "Dear Sophie. Thanks for asking about our plans for stores in Indianapolis . . ." and so forth. If there are more personal details, like "Fluffy has become a member of our family," Fluffy is also included.
- *Steal time.* I carry a BlackBerry device with me at all times, so I always have access to my e-mail—whether at home on the sofa or waiting for a plane at the airport. I maximize what would otherwise be wasted time by replying to Guest e-mail messages while waiting to do something else.
- *Acknowledge the effort.* I always thank my Guests for writing to me and tell them that I'm glad to help them. If I've been busy with other work and slower than normal to respond, I apologize for my lateness in answering the e-mail.
- *Keep organized records.* I save every Guest e-mail I get. Once I've sent a response, I file the e-mail by topic in special folders

in my e-mail management program. Suggestions for new store locations, for example, go into a "real estate" file by state and city. That way if the Guest writes to me again and references the first letter, I can easily find it. These e-mails also serve as a valuable database of Guest information and suggestions.

- *Check your spam folder.* Given the huge number of e-mail messages I get every day, I use a spam-blocking program to filter out the junk mail. Since legitimate e-mails are sometimes routed to the spam folder, I check it weekly to make sure I haven't missed any important messages from Guests or colleagues.

> *Some tricks of simplifying correspondence: create standardized responses, personalize every letter, and keep organized records.*

I do spend a great amount of time corresponding with Guests, but it's worth it. I view this task not as a chore, but as one of my most important jobs as Chief Executive Bear.

Guests provide me with valuable insights into the business. The people who write represent a good cross section of our customer base, young and old. They help me know what's going on every day in all of our stores around the world.

> *Responding to feedback is bound to make the angriest customer loyal. Ignoring their comments will make them even more angry and lead to lost business from countless others with the same frustrations.*

If your customers can take a few minutes out of their own busy schedules to write to you, you should certainly spare the small amount of time needed to reply.

After all, responding is bound to make even the angriest customer extremely loyal. By contrast, ignoring their comments will likely lead to lost business from them as well as countless others who no doubt have the same thoughts, suggestions, and frustrations.

Part Four

Creating an Incredible Experience

Make First Impressions Last

You never get a second chance to make a first impression.

This important life lesson is perhaps even more crucial in business. If you don't make a good first impression on your current and potential customers, they're likely to walk away and take their business elsewhere. And you'll have to work that much harder to win back their business in the future.

How important are first impressions at Build-A-Bear Workshop? So important that we have associates in every store who are responsible for ensuring that Guests have a good one. We call these people our First Impression Bears (FIBs).

If you don't make a good first impression, customers are likely to take their business elsewhere.

If you've been to our store, you've met an FIB. This is the Bear Builder associate who stands at the entrance, greets every Guest, and explains what Build-A-Bear Workshop is all about. Lots of times, they pass out free stickers or stroll around with a stuffed animal on skates.

The idea for having a First Impression Bear dates back to our first store. Ours wasn't just a brand-new business; it was an entirely new concept. People had never been to a place like this before.

As I was getting the company off the ground, many of my friends volunteered to work in shifts at the store. It immediately became clear from the questions and quizzical looks of our Guests that they didn't understand what we were selling or what they were supposed to do inside our stores.

So one of my friends, Ellen White, stationed herself at the entrance and talked to people as they walked by or came in, inviting them to play. In addition to being a great advocate for the business, my friend is a really nice person and a great businesswoman to boot! Her presence at the front door made Guests feel welcome. It created such a great first impression, we decided to station FIBs at every one of our stores. They're our version of the Wal-Mart greeter.

Being an FIB is one of the most important jobs in our company. All of our associates get special training in how to make a Guest's first impression of our business a positive one.

Some associates are better at the job than others, because there are those who are naturally outgoing. This is definitely a job best suited to a good-natured extrovert, and we try to station people with those talents at the entrance as often as possible. We count on these associates to make our Guests feel welcome and to bring passersby into the store.

> *You have to work much harder to earn back lost business.*

The second part of the job is particularly tricky. Part of being an FIB involves "reading" the Guests, figuring out their needs, and making suggestions to fit them.

Say an FIB spots a mom who is clearly in a rush shopping at the mall with her kids. We don't want that FIB to hijack the mom's time by luring her kids into the store to make a bear. But we would like for that FIB to give the kids some free stickers and invite the family to come back when they have more time. Again, it's about making a good first impression. We're hoping that when that mother has time to do something fun with her kids, she'll remember she was treated well at Build-A-Bear Workshop and will want to come back.

In any business, you have to pay attention to first impressions. And you must realize that there's more than one way to make a first impression on a customer. There are many ways people are first exposed to Build-A-Bear Workshop—through the malls they visit, our web site, television ads, community involvement, newspaper stories written about us, and our mobile store. We want everyone's initial exposure to our company to be positive, happy, and fun—all the things our brand represents.

Every company and businessperson has multiple opportunities to make a good first impression. If you are selling yourself and a service you provide, your first impression is made through your appearance and dress, your manner on the telephone, and your written communication. Does your manner instill confidence or cost you customers?

Here are a few other areas where you may be making a good (or bad) first impression on your customers.

Whatchamacallit

Does the name of your business convey the right image to your customers? Does it capture what your business is all about? It should.

> *Your appearance, dress, telephone manner, and written communications all impact how customers think of you.*

A few years back, the overnight delivery company once known as Federal Express officially shortened its name to FedEx. The purpose of the name change? Matching customers' first impressions with what the brand is all about.

Motley Fool analyst Todd Lebor explained FedEx's motivations well in a May 2001 article about the company, written at the time of the change. "FedEx is in the midst of an image remake," he reported. "It recently changed its name from FDX Corp. to FedEx Corp. . . . Federal Express is too long. It doesn't convey the speed of FedEx. People are too busy to say Federal Express. If someone needed to get a package out ASAP, precious time could be lost on all those syllables.

"Fred Smith, FedEx's founder, long-time chairman, president, and CEO . . . understands that each truck, drop box, and uniform seen on the street is a brand impression. Passing up the opportunity to create a favorable impression is not only stupid, it's bad business. So, what's in name? Only the last chance to make a (positive) first impression."

Appearances Matter

Think about the first things your customers see when they visit your business. The customer experience doesn't begin at your front door. It begins in the parking lot. Is yours easy to enter and exit? Or do your customers have to make a left turn across two lanes of busy traffic to get to your company? If you think these things don't matter, you're mistaken. There are plenty of examples of businesses that have failed because of bad or hard-to-access locations.

Whether customers can find a place to park will also color their first impressions, as will the cleanliness of your parking lot. Signage also counts. What do you think of businesses with letters missing from their signs, misspelled words on their buildings, or burned-out marquees? Probably not much.

> *Customers begin to experience your company even before stepping through the front door.*

Martha Stewart Is Right—Hospitality Is a Good Thing

This is good for my business, but a sad fact for the retail industry: Build-A-Bear Workshop is unique in how it greets its Guests. Few other retailers welcome customers to their stores, even if there's an employee standing near the entrance. (Wal-Mart is the obvious exception.) I can't count the number of times I have walked into a store and been ignored. How much effort would it take for a sales clerk who is folding T-shirts near the front door to smile and say hello to every customer who walks in? Here's the straight truth from someone who knows: Smiles and kind words don't cost a cent, but they mean a great deal to customers.

This same philosophy applies to other businesses. How you greet and treat those who do business with you will impact how well you do in business.

Be cognizant of how you welcome folks to your business. What does your lobby look like? Are there chairs or sofas for people to sit on while they wait? Does your receptionist say hello? Or does he or she dispense with pleasantries altogether, preferring curt phrases like "Next" or "Take a number"?

In these tougher economic times, some businesses have gotten rid of receptionists to cut costs. If that's you, think about what this says to the people who visit you. If there is no one posted at the front door to tend to their needs, how else can you make visitors feel welcome? If a telephone is your receptionist, is it easy to use? Or do visitors have to dial multiple numbers before finding someone to help them?

One Moment Please

We all know how frustrating it is to be put on hold indefinitely. What's even worse is getting trapped in an automated phone system (for questions about your bill, press 1; for questions about your service, press 2; to report an outage, press 3 . . .).

What do your customers experience when they call you? And how genuine is it to put people on hold automatically by playing a message that says, "We very much value your business and apologize for the delay in answering your call"? If you really value my business, you shouldn't put me on hold in the first place!

Replacements, Ltd., an Internet and mail-order company in North Carolina that sells hard-to-find china, crystal, and silverware, has a rule that customers shouldn't have to wait longer than seven seconds before their call is answered by a real person. How do they do it? Replacements has a large call-center staff. But if they're busy, customer phone calls roll over to the remaining office staff. These people, including the corporate executives, stop what they're doing to answer the phone and take customer orders. Replacements is a business driven by telephone sales, and the CEO doesn't want to give his customers a reason to hang up and call the competition. So, he sometimes answers the phone himself. That's quite a way to make a first impression.

At every touch point you have with your customers, focus on making a good impression. Some customers may give you a second chance to win their business, but many others will not. And if you fail to make a good impression the second time around, your chances of winning that customer are even slimmer. Fail a third time and it's like baseball: You're out of the game.

When it comes to impressing customers, my best advice is this: Do it right the first time.

Turn Every Day into a Holiday

The average toy store records 40 to 50 percent of its sales—and an even bigger share of its profits—during the Christmas holiday season. The same is true for many other retailers, from jewelers to clothing stores. But that's not the case at Build-A-Bear Workshop. The reason? For us, every day is a holiday.

For starters, we specialize in helping guests of all ages celebrate their birthdays—and birthdays take place seven days a week, 365 days a year. For most, birthdays are the most important personal holiday of all. That's certainly true for me, and has been ever since I was a little girl. After all, it's your own special day, when all of the attention is focused on *you*. What's more, people tend to spend more on birthday gifts than on holiday presents, leading to a bigger overall sale.

Tie your product or service in with the celebration of one's birthday.

Since launching our Build-A-Party program, we have become a popular place to host parties for scouts, school classes, and all types of other celebrations. But we're not limited to just children and teens. Corporations schedule parties for their customers, employees, and families as well. Most store locations are booked solid for parties throughout the year. In essence, these Guests make reservations to shop in our stores, and they bring a sizable group of friends with them. In addition to being a privilege I hold dear and a way for word-of-mouth marketing to really take hold, these prescheduled party visits are also very advantageous from a cash flow and schedule planning perspective.

Therefore, if there's a way to tie your product or service in with the celebration of a customer's birthday, I highly recommend it. For instance, many restaurants offer a free birthday meal, knowing people often come in groups to eat out on this special occasion (and they usually order extra drinks and dessert to mark the event). As a result, what seems to be a free offer is really a very lucrative business proposition for the restaurant.

We send most of our younger Guests a card and $5 gift certificate on their birthday. A large percentage of them redeem these cards within days of receiving them. We also e-mail birthday cards to our Guests' bears (or bunnies or frogs), which include a gift certificate the furry creature's owner can use to get a free accessory. (Trust me: When Guests come in, they usually leave with much more than the free gift for their prized plush friend!)

> *Wishing someone a happy birthday gives you a perfect reason to get your company's name in front of your loyal customers when they're in a good mood.*

Even if you're not in the kind of business where people would be apt to come and personally celebrate on your premises, you should still get to know the birthday of each customer and offer some kind of "birthday special," which can be announced by regular mail, phone, or even e-mail. Perhaps you can provide 10 percent off on services in honor of the special day. Not only are you apt to see a huge response, but wishing someone a happy birthday also gives you a perfect reason to get your company's name and offerings in front of your most loyal customers, and it's guaranteed to put a smile on their faces. Plus, there's no better time to reach out to prospects than when they're in a good mood!

You really don't have to offer more than a simple birthday card to earn the admiration of your customers. Nobody knows that better than Southwest Airlines. Several years ago, the discount carrier began sending out birthday cards to each member of its Rapid Rewards frequent-flier program. According to the company, it gets more complimentary letters from passengers about this one unexpected perk than any other, not to mention loyalty. After all, when was the last time you heard of a big impersonal airline sending out birthday cards?

Chico's, the specialty apparel chain catering to women over 35, sends a birthday coupon to its Passport members for use during their birthday month. It knows customers are busy, so they have up to 30 days to use it. Even older women care about their birthdays!

There are other ways to make every day a holiday. For instance, most toy introductions occur in the second half of the year. Not at Build-A-Bear Workshop. We launch a new Beary Limited edition item on the day *after* every holiday. In turn, we've created an event for our Guests to anticipate that isn't based on discounts or sales. Instead, it's driven by what I believe customers of all businesses are really looking for—newness.

We introduced our first Beary Limited edition Centennial Teddy Bear in 1999, which was followed by another new edition for the following five years. The series commemorated the 100th anniversary of the teddy bear in 2002.

Many people ask whether I miss the fashion business. How could I? Fashion is what teddy bears are all about, and we come up with new outfits and accessories for every holiday. In February we turn into the "Love Stuff Headquarters," complete with our own unique "Hugday" fashions. In the summer, our bears, bunnies, and other animals get decked out in beachwear. In October, Halloween costumes for our furry friends are very popular. Because we design and develop our own products, we are better able to control our own destiny and get just the right look for the occasion.

So, by all means, don't make your sales a slave to the calendar. Take control of your own destiny by building promotions around every holiday, including the most perpetual one of all—birthdays.

Emulate the Five Pillars of Success

A table needs four legs to be sturdy, but a business needs five. It's what our outside marketing consultant, Barkley Evergreen & Partners, calls the "Five Pillars" of success. I like to think of these pillars as the essential components of any business. They also represent the five choices you must make when mapping out a strategy for your business.

> *The five pillars are price, convenience, product, customer service, and overall experience.*

The five pillars, in no particular order of importance, are price, convenience, product innovation, customer service, and overall experience. To be viable and competitive, your company must offer some measure of each component. Your pricing must be such that consumers find value in your products when comparing them to the competition. You have to provide some level of convenience, so it's

Primary Pillars of Some of Today's Leading Companies					
	Price	Convenience	Product	Service	Experience
Disney			✔		✔
Chico's			✔	✔	
Wal-Mart	✔	✔			
Target	✔	✔	✔		
Build-A-Bear Workshop			✔	✔	✔
Sharper Image			✔		
Apple Computer			✔		✔
QuikTrip		✔			
Starbucks			✔		✔
Southwest Airlines	✔	✔			
Advanced Auto Parts				✔	
Dunkin Donuts		✔	✔		
Ritz-Carlton				✔	✔

easy to do business with you. Your product must be desirable and something people need. You need to offer a high level of customer service, and the overall experience of working with you must compare favorably to that offered by others in the industry.

Every company must meet the threshold level for each of the five pillars in order to stay in business. But success takes more than that.

Depending on your own professional goals, you must choose two or three of the five pillars to focus on without fail. Ask yourself the same sorts of questions you probably pondered when deciding on your college major. What do I do best? What choice is likely to do the most good for me financially? In what area can I make a contribution that others can't? Selecting the most important pillars for your company forces you to differentiate your brand in a meaningful way.

At Build-A-Bear Workshop, I think we do well at delivering on each of the pillars. But the three that we really concentrate on are overall experience, customer service, and product, and they're the factors that make us different from any of the other toy stores and/or other bear-making retailers out there.

> *Every company must meet the threshold level for each of the five pillars in order to stay in business.*

You can easily identify brands that excel at delivering on at least one of the five pillars. For instance, which companies are known for delivering convenience? QuikTrip stores and Walgreens come to mind. They both also offer good product selection, reasonable prices, friendly customer service, and a relatively pleasant shopping experience. But the standout feature of both of these brands is convenience. Most Walgreens stores are open 24 hours a day, seven days a week, and the pharmacies stay open later than most competitors. QuikTrip's 450 locations are located near major highways and interstates and offer conveniences like clean bathrooms and a wide selection of the good food and beverages travelers really appreciate.

Wal-Mart's primary pillar is price. The chain, which also excels at convenience, has rolled back prices so that its name is synonymous with good deals. Rarely can you find merchandise priced more affordably than at Wal-Mart. That reality contributed to Target becoming more fashion-oriented, putting its emphasis on another pillar—product. And it also probably contributed to Kmart's business challenges because that retailer isn't associated with any particular pillar at all.

> *Determine where your business stands on each of the five pillars, and identify those areas you most need to improve upon.*

When I think of product innovation, several companies come to mind. Sony and Apple, for instance, are always on the cutting edge in terms of home electronics and computers. What product in recent memory has done as much to revolutionize consumer habits and an industry as Apple's iPod? In the retail world, The Sharper Image stands out for its products. You can always find unusual gifts there. The company is known for stocking items not found in other stores. It's the sort of stuff that makes you want to slap your forehead and say, "Why didn't I think of that?"

Who's focused on the service pillar? I'd say Nordstrom, which has an unparalleled return policy and employees who are some of the friendliest and most attentive you'll find anywhere. Advanced Auto Parts is another good example. Once they ring up a sale, employees are more than happy to help you with minor maintenance and repairs, like installing a new battery or replacing the windshield wiper blades.

Finally, we come to the last pillar—overall experience. Disney, my favorite company ever (besides Build-A-Bear Workshop, of course), makes the list, as does Starbucks, another brand I've modeled my business on.

As you can see from these examples, successful companies really go to the extreme in order to deliver on the pillar that is most critical to their business strategy. In our case, we have created a special experience and we deliver that experience consistently. We also continue to innovate and introduce new products. We bring out new animals every season, and additional clothing selections are added every time fashions change. Our goal is not to offer the least expensive plush toy, but our animals are reasonably priced and Guests certainly consider them to be a good value. Unlike Wal-Mart or McDonald's, we don't aspire to be on every street corner, but we do like to offer the convenience of being in the best malls alongside other stores where our Guests frequently shop. In other words, we care about all five pillars, but our brand strategy dictates that we concentrate on three and deliver with excellence on those every time.

> *If your performance is lacking in any area, ratchet it up so that you're at least meeting the expectations set by the marketplace.*

Consider the five pillars as they relate to your own business. Your very first step is to determine where you stand on each one. If your performance is lacking in any area, you must ratchet it up so that you're at least meeting the expectations set by the marketplace. Once you're at par, so to speak, you can choose a single pillar—or two or three—to emphasize and build your brand identity around.

Keep Inventory in Check

I bet you never knew that being an entrepreneur requires psychic abilities. Well, at least that's what it feels like sometimes. You often seem to need a crystal ball, in order to look into the future and therefore make smarter decisions. This is particularly true when it comes to planning and buying inventory.

Inventory should match demand as closely as possible.

When you're just starting out, it's hard to anticipate demand and determine precisely what quantities of each product to have on hand for your business. I can only imagine what restaurateurs go through as they're ordering food for opening night. How do they know how much to order? They want to be able to fill every plate, without having too much excess. In the restaurant biz, you can't serve leftovers, and raw ingredients spoil pretty quickly.

Thankfully, most products don't perish like food, so an inventory glut won't usually mean literally throwing money away. But figuratively speaking, it's the same thing. You won't make money if your products just sit on the shelves, yet if those shelves are empty, your register will equally run dry. That's why inventory should match demand as closely as possible.

How do you accomplish this? Through trial and error, and by making quick adjustments to correct those errors. Of course, it's also important to have a good inventory control system that tracks what's selling—and what's not—so you can make smart buying decisions.

> *It's important to have good inventory control systems in place so you can make smart buying decisions.*

Even with my extensive experience in retail, I wasn't quite sure how much inventory to order for our first store opening. I bought what I thought was a six-month supply based on our business plan. But it soon became clear by our diminishing stock that we would sell out much quicker than expected. That's when I called our suppliers and rush-ordered more products to fill the ever-widening gap between supply and demand.

Since you can't sell air, sometimes we fly things in at an additional cost in order to get the products on the shelves and in our Guests' hands quicker. We did this a few years ago when we introduced a pink poncho for our bears. Demand exceeded even our most optimistic projections, and our stores were constantly selling out. As soon as we recognized how popular the item was, we had our supplier make and send us more. The rush job cost extra, slightly cutting into our profit margins, but I think the added expense was worth it. We sold many more than we could have otherwise. I'd rather reap smaller profits on one item than disappoint a

Guest by being sold out of the bear or the outfit that he or she is looking for. That's one reason we keep our assortment narrow— limited to only about 300 to 400 products. It makes managing inventory much easier.

What lessons can you take from my experiences? First, if you're in an inventory-driven business, know that it's okay to miss the mark on inventory initially. Make your best estimate of how much product you'll need, based on your knowledge of the industry and your researched assessment of demand in your particular product category. When launching a new business or product, it can be difficult to accurately project demand. Make a best guess, then quickly correct and learn from any mistakes. (And don't forget to include a mistake budget line as well.)

> *It's better to reap smaller profits on a particular item than to disappoint customers.*

That's also lesson number two: Learn from past experiences. We use sales data from previous store openings and product launches as our guide when preparing for new locations. Additionally, every week I review a list of our 20 best-selling items by department in each store. This helps me make all kinds of decisions about product innovation, marketing, and inventory planning—including how much of each item we need and where.

To me, it's just common sense to learn from how you did things last time so you can do it even better on the next go-round. Apparently, many businesses don't take that approach. When I shop, I always browse through the markdown racks. They are invariably filled with lots of small sizes, especially 2s and 4s. I can go back to the same store, season after season, and see the same inventory mistakes repeated—a glut of small sizes and a shortage of larger ones. I bet these retailers order the same amount of merchandise in each size, without paying attention to actual demand patterns or to the fact that the average woman in America wears a size 14, not a size 2. That fact alone should be an indication that stores need to stock more larger than smaller sizes.

> *Let past experiences be your guide when estimating future demand.*

If you work in the retail business, I encourage you to check out your competitors' markdowns and redlined merchandise. You can make similar observations in the service industry. What you find will reveal valuable information about what doesn't sell so you can plan your own inventory accordingly.

Finally, embrace the technology that is available to help you with this task. Wal-Mart probably has the best inventory control system in the world. Every time a customer buys a product, information on that sale is relayed to a distribution center so the stock can be replenished overnight. Luckily, there are many commercially available software programs that will help you manage your inventory as effectively as Wal-Mart does. The key is choosing a solution that integrates point-of-sale activity to your back-office software, so you can clearly see which items are selling and need to be reordered, and which aren't and may need to be discounted.

> *Pay attention to what your competitors are marking down for insight into what you might want to order less of.*

Inventory management isn't an easy job, and never will be. Even with the best tools and research, it's impossible to gauge consumer demand with precision. That's why it's crucial to maintain flexibility, so you can make adjustments to your offerings in order to match market demands. Of course, we all hope to achieve that perfect balance—having just enough inventory. But accomplishing this is harder than walking a tightrope in high heels. Therefore, the choice often boils down to having either too much or too little. Because my ultimate focus is on making Guests happy, I prefer to err on the side of having too much. The reason? It's much easier to get rid of surplus merchandise than to the change the mind-set of a disappointed Guest.

Pay Attention
to Packaging

There is perhaps no packaging more iconic than the Tiffany & Co. robin's-egg-blue box, which was first introduced in 1837. Through more than a century and a half, that box has come to represent quality, luxury, exclusivity, style, and sophistication—characteristics customers also associate with Tiffany's products. The box, which is as bright as a dyed Easter egg, has helped to establish Tiffany & Co. as a premium brand. The company is therefore able to command a higher price for its products.

> *Packaging should be a priority for every company.*

The Tiffany example proves just how much impact packaging can have. Tiffany's blue boxes represent a very small incremental cost for the company, but they make a huge statement to its customers.

I believe that packaging should be a priority for every company. It really matters, even if you're not selling something that can be put into a box or bag. A resume is packaging. So is a marketing brochure, and the clothing you wear when meeting with a potential client or going on a job interview. After all, these are all highly visible ways of promoting your brand.

> *A resume, marketing brochure, and clothing are all forms of packaging.*

Packaging can serve a variety of purposes.

- *It can be functional.* At Macaroni Grill, leftovers are packed in aluminum pans that can be popped in the oven for reheating. The top even provides instructions for how to warm up certain dishes.
- *It can be unique.* In the 1970s, L'eggs hosiery outsold the competition by packaging its pantyhose in a plastic egg.
- *It can make a style statement.* Apple's sales exploded after introducing its colorful line of iMac computers.
- *It can be practical.* Think of the Toilet Duck brand of bathroom cleaner from SC Johnson. This bottled cleanser has a curved neck, which makes it easier to clean under the rim of the toilet bowl.
- *It can be user-friendly.* Target made headlines after changing the shape of its prescription drug bottles, creating easier-to-read labels, and adding a color-coding system.
- *It can be another way to reinforce your brand.* Among the in-flight snacks served by discount carrier JetBlue Airways are blue-colored potato chips.

When done right, packaging is a great forum for advertising your business.

- **It can make a statement about the quality of your merchandise.** Designer handbags are often placed into cotton dust bags before being slipped into heavy-duty shopping sacks.
- **It can make your customers feel special.** Chico's makes its packages look like presents. Every item is wrapped in the company's signature tissue paper and tied with curly ribbon.
- **It can help you stand out from the competition.** Rather than the standard plastic case, the DVD for the television show *Northern Exposure* came zipped in an orange quilted parka.
- **It can be a badge of honor.** There are some packages, like the Tiffany blue box, that consumers covet and carry proudly. Have you ever seen someone try to hide a shopping bag from Saks Fifth Avenue?
- **It can offer convenience to your customers.** Frito-Lay now sells Go Snacks, chips packaged in small canisters that fit in an automobile cup holder.
- **It can be another forum for advertising your business.** Our Cub Condo carrying cases and Beararmoire cardboard closets are literally walking billboards for our brand. Kids see other kids carrying them around the mall, and they're drawn to our stores.

Clever and creative packaging gives you a chance to distinguish your products from those of the competition.

When deciding how to package your own products, remember the Tiffany blue box and these other great examples. Clever and creative packaging gives you yet another chance to distinguish your products from those of the competition. In addition, it can be a relatively easy and inexpensive way to reinforce your brand, and also makes a statement about how you feel about your customers.

Offer an Escape
from the Ordinary

As you already know, I'm a huge fan of Walt Disney and have tried to model my professional life after his.

In my opinion, Disneyland and Disney World have really earned their reputation as the "happiest places on earth." Disney sets the standard for great customer service and entertainment. As soon as you pay your admission fee, it's good-bye to the ordinary and hello to the extraordinary as all your cares dash away in this imaginary world.

The Disney parks are truly like no other places on earth. They are unparalleled in their entertainment value, but not in their ability to deliver an extraordinary experience. It's my belief that every company can offer its customers an escape from the ordinary, perhaps not on the same scale as Disney, but with small, inexpensive, and unexpected gestures.

Accomplishing this is quite simple. You need only do things that aren't standard in your industry and aren't expected at your price point. Instead, emphasize those small touches that signal to your customers that they're special and appreciated. Your goal should be to elicit a smile and the reaction, *I didn't know you did that.*

My local car wash is a perfect example of this principle in action. Like most car washes, this one has an indoor waiting room where customers can relax while their cars are being cleaned. This waiting room provides more than the ordinary selection of shopworn magazines. There's also an extensive selection of greeting cards for sale, and every time I take my car for a wash and wax, I find a card (or several) that I must buy for some occasion. This carwash does one other decidedly unordinary thing. It gives every customer a bag of goodies—breath mints, air freshener, and car-cleaning wipes—as a little thank-you gift for the business. How extraordinary—and extraordinarily simple.

In my job, I travel a lot and stay in a variety of hotels, from budget to luxury. When I stay in an inexpensive hotel, I don't expect much beyond a clean room and comfortable bed. Yet I've been pleasantly surprised by the hospitable touches offered by some moderate-priced hotels—things like free homemade cookies, bright shiny apples in the lobby, and luxurious-feeling down pillows and comforters. They go beyond what is ordinarily offered at hotels of that price range.

> *Every company can offer its customers an escape from the ordinary with small, inexpensive, and unexpected gestures.*

While we're on the subject of hotels, I'd like to share with you another example of beyond-ordinary service that was passed along by a friend.

A Kentucky businessman was traveling to North Carolina for a furniture industry trade show. The only room he could find was at the Elk Inn, a motor lodge in the tiny town of Elkin, about 90 miles away from where the show was being held. It cost just $40 a night.

When the man arrived at the motel, it was pretty much what he expected—an old-fashioned motor lodge, simply decorated yet, thankfully, clean. The owner was a pretty young woman who had returned to her hometown for a break from the corporate world.

The following morning, the man informed the innkeeper that he might need the room for a second night. "No problem," she said, for there were no other guests scheduled to stay at the motel that week. "But if you're not coming back, call me or I'll worry," the innkeeper told her guest. I don't know about you, but I've never gotten that kind of consideration at even the most expensive hotels I've stayed in.

The businessman wound up staying another night at the Elk Inn. When he arrived back at the motel late that second night, he was surprised to see a light glowing through his window. "Oh no," he thought. "She's rented my room to someone else or let another guest in there." But when he unlocked the door, he discovered something quite extraordinary. The considerate innkeeper had turned on his bedside lamp and turned down the covers on the bed, service you wouldn't expect for $40 a night.

Unlike most other stores, we don't just ring up merchandise at Build-A-Bear Workshop. We sell an experience. This fact alone puts us in a separate category from every other merchant in the mall. We are, by definition, an escape from the ordinary.

No matter what your business, you can find ways to maximize the customer experience by replacing the common with the extraordinary. You're limited only by your imagination.

Emphasize those small touches that signal to your customers that they're special and appreciated.

I don't frequent tanning salons. But if I did, I'd want to go to a place like The Palms Tanning Resort, which has three locations in Colorado.

Most tanning salons are pretty bare-bones operations. Customers are ushered into tiny, sparsely decorated rooms, sometimes no bigger than a closet, where they soak up ultraviolet rays in tanning beds that would be more aptly named tanning coffins.

But the owners of The Palms took some cues from the spa industry and designed their business around relaxation and escape from everyday life. The company's tanning salons look and feel like tropical islands, complete with white sand beaches instead of traditional floors. Customers walk through sandstone caves and past waterfalls before being escorted into private tanning huts and bungalows named for and modeled after such tropical locales as Hawaii, Fiji, Jamaica, the Bahamas, Bora Bora, and Tahiti.

As you can see from this example, you don't have to create something new to offer your customers an escape from the ordinary. You just have to add your own personal touch, twist a concept just enough to make it unique, and make over the gold standard into something even better.

The founders of *USA Today* did an incredible job of creating a newspaper that was unlike any other in the nation, in terms of content and appearance. Now *USA Today*'s design has been copied and co-opted by many other publications. When it first debuted, *USA Today* was the only burst of color at newsstands. The rest of the competition was awash in gray. The newspaper's design emphasizes color, photography, and design. The stories are written from a national, rather than a local, perspective. And they're informative yet concise, deliberately short enough to read on the subway or in between meetings. (Not surprisingly, most of the competition has now followed suit by using color as well, at least in select sections of the paper.)

Maximize the customer experience by replacing the common with the extraordinary.

When I think about businesses that have succeeded in offering their customers an escape from the ordinary, many of them are in very traditional industries. Like *USA Today*, they've found their niche by catering to time-strapped individuals. A dry cleaning business is ordinary, but one that offers free pickup and delivery goes beyond what's normally expected. Ditto for quick-lube and windshield repair businesses that come to you, instead of the other way around, to work on your car.

If we didn't offer Guests a chance to make their own stuffed animals, we'd be like any other toy store. But Build-A-Bear Workshop is unique. Although we didn't invent making your own teddy bear, we popularized a whole concept in children's retailing.

How will you make your mark as a pioneer?

Part Five

Using Essential Marketing Strategies

Be a Great Brand

What is a brand?

Surprisingly, the definition means the same thing in the corporate world as it does on a cattle ranch.

A brand is a lasting imprint you leave on the marketplace.

A brand is a lasting imprint, the mark you leave on the marketplace. It is your company's reputation, culture, utter essence—indeed, its DNA. It is much more than a slogan. It's a promise your company makes and fulfills every day.

When creating your brand, follow the examples set by the other great brands out there like Disney, Coca-Cola, Maytag, Starbucks, Nike, and Kellogg's.

What does Build-A-Bear Workshop have in common with these

terrific companies? Most importantly, we share an emotional bond with our Guests. They know what we're all about, and they trust us because we've earned their confidence through good service and honesty. In addition, like these other top brands, we offer Guests a consistent experience time and again.

Usually, your brand can be summarized in just a few words, many of which describe feelings. Disney means family. Nike equals personal triumph and athletic excellence. Maytag stands for reliability. Build-A-Bear Workshop stores are known for offering wholesome family fun. Some of our Guests even say we epitomize love.

> *Think of your brand as a promise your company makes and fulfills every day.*

When's the time to start defining and building your brand? From the very start. I outlined my ideas for the Build-A-Bear Workshop brand when writing my business plan. And like a business plan, your brand blueprint serves as a guide for every decision you make and every strategy you undertake.

> *The time to start defining your brand is when you begin planning your business.*

We initially spent several hundreds of thousands of dollars on brand building. We hired the Adrienne Weiss Company to translate my ideas for the brand into such visual elements as in-store signs, interior designs, displays, and graphics. This process also included creating the company's unique language—that is, our product names, trademarked in-store station names, and our Bearisms.

Costly as it was, this has been our best investment ever in terms of the value we received for the money spent.

Brands, like countries, have their own unique cultures and language. We think of ourselves as a country with our own language, rituals, and traditions. Starbucks is a great example of this. Starbucks positioned itself as an expert purveyor of high-quality and carefully brewed coffee. Its employees are not simply servers; they are baristas with special training in coffee grinding and brewing techniques. Beverages are not served in ordinary sizes of small, medium, and large, but rather in tall, grande, and venti cups.

More than anything, though, a brand is a company's soul. Being a brand means letting the outside world know about the inner workings and culture of your business. Of course, this involves much more than lip service. You can't just say to the world what you are; you have to demonstrate it by your actions. That's the hardest part. Your brand's values must be conveyed in everything you do, from your hiring processes to your dealings with suppliers. Employees must understand these values, believe in them, and mirror them. In evaluating the strengths of your own brand, ask yourself one important question: Are you who you say you are in every aspect of what you do?

> *Brands, like countries, have their own cultures, traditions, and languages.*

Being a brand is a lot like having personal integrity. Saying you are an honest and fair person doesn't make it true. You have to live with integrity seven days a week, 52 weeks a year. That means being straightforward about both the big and small things. You can't have integrity if you're unfaithful to your spouse or steal your neighbor's newspaper.

> *More than anything, a brand is a company's soul.*

Remember that branding is a way of being that flows through every aspect of the company, like blood through the body. It is reflected in your products, employees, partnerships, culture, policies, and business strategies. When you decide to become a brand, and not just a business, you create the guidebook for everything you do in the future.

The Best
Advertising Is Free

Paid advertising is an effective way to spread the word about your business. But the absolute best advertising is free. It happens when one customer heaps praise on your company to another person.

> *The most powerful advertising happens when one customer heaps praise on your company to another.*

My company uses traditional advertising, and we've been doing so more in recent years in order to tap into new customer markets. But we've found that the most powerful and effective way to advertise our business is by having our existing Guests do it for us. Their enthusiasm for our brand and the experience they have when they visit us is infinitely more effective in driving new Guests to our stores than any commercials or print advertisements. In fact, at least one-third of our new Guests hear about us from a friend or family member.

To generate your own positive word-of-mouth free advertising—the buzz that is so crucial to success—you must cultivate customer evangelists (a term coined by authors Ben McConnell and Jackie Huba)—or as we call them, "spokesbears." These are, in essence, your most loyal customers who passionately recommend you to their friends, family, and even strangers. Their loyalty is rooted in something deeper than the fact that you're more convenient or less expensive than the competition. They are loyal because they believe in you and what you sell or what you do, and feel a deeper connection to your business than they do to others.

> *To generate positive word-of-mouth advertising, you must cultivate customer evangelists.*

Evangelism is where advertising and marketing intertwine. How you market to your customers and connect with them will determine the frequency and tenor of the free advertising you receive. And while you may save advertising dollars, you can't scrimp on spending when it comes to customer service if you want to achieve good buzz. That's right: Free advertising will cost you, in that you must invest in ways to forge deeper connections with your customers and exceed their expectations on a daily basis.

> *Evangelism is where advertising and marketing intertwine.*

I believe *The Bear Necessities of Business* provides the blueprint for how to create buzz. Follow the strategies I outline, and you're sure to have customers talking about what makes your business so extraordinary. That said, there is one primary way to get people talking about your company in a positive way.

Show your customers that they are important. That should be reflected in the way they're treated during every interaction, whether they spend a dollar or a million dollars. To create true loyalty, you must connect with them on an emotional level, not just through their brains or pocketbooks. They have to feel welcomed, appreciated, valued, and respected as more than just a sale.

I think that half of the buzz about Build-A-Bear Workshop comes from the fact that we stand out in a crowd. Granted, we're a different retail concept, and our stores are both brightly colored and well lit. But what really distinguishes us from other stores in the mall is not *what* we do, but *how* we do it. Our mission is to delight and entertain our Guests, to make sure that everyone who visits leaves our stores feeling better than they did when they walked in. We're one of the few retailers that consistently gives away freebies (things like bear-themed stickers) whether someone buys from us or not. And we make a point of repeating a very simple, yet meaningful, phrase hundreds of times a day: "Thank you." Think of how many businesses forget to say that!

> *Don't scrimp on spending when it comes to customer service.*

Our Guests tell me over and over again that these small touches make a big difference to them. We know these are the characteristics they laud when they tell their friends about us, and that's why we focus so much of our attention on them. We understand the touchstones for our Guests, and we strive to consistently go beyond their already high expectations for us.

It's also important to turn mistakes made in dealing with your customers into opportunities. Botch an interaction, and you have two basic options for responding to the problem. The outcomes are as divergent as Robert Frost's paths in the woods.

> *The best way to get people buzzing about your business is to show them they are important.*

You can let the mistake stand and allow that customer to walk away unsatisfied. Make this choice, and that person is likely to hold a grudge for a long time. Plus, chances are he or she will share the bad experience with others. I've heard people repeat the same bad-service stories at cocktail parties for years. That's free advertising, but not the kind you want. Think about all the negative publicity Hermès received after denying Oprah Winfrey after-hours entry to one of its stores. Oprah has more power than most when it comes to swaying consumer opinions. But within our own circle of friends and family, we all exert similar influence. No amount of money spent on traditional advertising can make up for a customer's bad experience, nor will it turn their opinion of you around.

But if you follow that second path, by finding a way to turn the mistake into a positive for the customer, you have a good chance of transforming that person into a loyal evangelist for your company. My philosophy is that when you wow one Guest by treating him or her better than he or she ever expected to be treated, you'll wow nine more as well.

One more point on this concept of making mistakes work for you, instead of against you, is that it seems to be human nature to let bad experiences fester and perpetuate. I can't tell you how many times I've walked into a business and heard the people who work there harping about some troublesome customer they've just had to deal with. I understand the need to vent, but when you do this in front of other customers, you're degrading their experience. You've lost yet another opportunity to convert someone from customer to evangelist—and to cash in on free, positive advertising. Remember, every customer is an opportunity to spread the word about your business to many more people.

There are other ways to generate buzz and free advertising, and Build-A-Bear Workshop employs them all. We stage grand opening events that draw huge crowds, and we give our time and money to help local and national charities. We also send out press releases so newspapers and television stations will publicize things that are going on at our company.

Never forget to say, "Thank you."

These strategies result in blips of free advertising. But none of these methods provide the same sustained and hypereffective buzz that we receive from our evangelists, those Guests with whom we've forged a personal connection.

Target Your Pitches

Another very valuable form of free advertising comes from getting members of the media to do stories about you and your company. In my book, this kind of coverage is priceless, and has far more impact than advertising. Imagine how much more people are likely to trust something seen on *Oprah* or the *Today* show than what they hear or see in an advertisement.

Getting positive media coverage is priceless.

Think about what it's like to work as a reporter for a newspaper. Every day begins with thousands of inches of newsprint that must be filled with informative and compelling stories that both educate and inform your readers. In addition to the five essential questions that all reporters learn to ask in journalism school—who, what, when, where, and why—there's a sixth component that every media story must have, whether it's in a newspaper,

208

magazine, or on television: the "so what?" factor. In other words, why is this newsworthy?

This is the first question any reporter is going to ask when you pitch a story about your business. So what? What makes this a story? What makes this interesting? What is unique about this? What will make people want to read this or watch 60 seconds of video about it? What about your company makes it worth the newsprint or airtime?

For some legitimate reasons—and others unfounded—there are people who don't like reporters and couldn't imagine anything worse than winding up in the newspaper or on the news. However, I've always had pretty good relationships with members of the media. Maybe that's because I understand how hard their jobs really are. I studied journalism at the University of Georgia, but fate led me to retail, a career to which I'm much better suited. Throughout the years, I've met some reporters whom I really clicked with, and others I didn't like as much. Personalities and personal opinion aside, I've learned how helpful the media can be in telling our story, spreading the word about an event, and bringing people to our stores.

People respond to what they read in print and see on television news, especially when it gets reported by someone they trust and admire. Therefore, if you shun media coverage, you're missing out on an effective and relatively inexpensive promotional source. And, as you've learned throughout this book, it's smart to use every tool available when building your brand.

> *The first question reporters will ask is, "So what?" You need to give them a good reason to do a story about you and your business.*

How does any company get media coverage? One reporter and relationship at a time. And, like anything else, these relationships take time to build.

You're probably aware that we have received a lot of national and local media coverage. None of it was by accident. We worked hard for each of those hits and, most importantly, we planned ahead. Once we know when and where we're opening stores, we proactively seek media coverage by doing the public relations (PR) basics of contacting all the media outlets in those markets and by sending out solid and interesting press kits, cleverly packaged in our Cub Condo carrying cases with a cuddly teddy bear messenger included inside. We follow up on those press kits with telephone calls and targeted story ideas (the follow-up is absolutely crucial, because reporters get so many things sent their way). In our first two years of business, we tried to set up face-to-face meetings to tell their reporters more about the company and explain our unique concept. Now that we're better known, that isn't always necessary.

We also make it easy for the media to cover us by giving them good story ideas. That's the real dividing line between companies, big and small, that get media coverage and those that don't. Most reporters are not going to respond to a lackluster pitch or boring press release, which they get plenty of.

Here is an example of an ineffective PR pitch. The scenario itself is fictional, but it is based in fact.

A reporter's telephone rings.

"Hello. *Daily News*. How may I help you?"

"Well, I was hoping you might be interested in doing a write-up about my business. I sell used cars. I know there are a lot of other car lots in town, and we're pretty much like the rest of them. But I advertise in the paper; I spend a lot of money with you every week. We've been open for about six months now, and I thought an article might help our sales."

> *Follow-up is a critical step to getting media coverage.*

Can you count the mistakes? First of all, this pitch fails to satisfy the "so what?" factor. Among other things, it's old news. What's newsworthy about a six-month-old car dealership that, at least as presented here, is no different from the competition? The next mistake is expecting quid pro quo. At any reputable news organization, the advertising department has no control over what the news department covers. Media outlets aim for objectivity, and that means treating advertisers and nonadvertisers fairly, applying the same standards when writing good or bad news stories. No matter how much you spend on advertising, you won't be able to buy coverage by a reputable newspaper, magazine, or television station.

I'm going to come back to that fictional scenario a little bit later, but right now I want to talk about the basics of good, effective PR.

Have you ever interviewed a potential job candidate who was clueless about what your company does, what you stand for, and how you fit in the marketplace? I bet you didn't hire that person, because they didn't do their research in advance. Reporters feel the same way when people approach them with story ideas without first doing a bit of homework. Most reporters cover specific beats, and that means they write only about certain topics. Your local newspaper probably has someone who writes about religion, another who covers schools, another who follows county government, another who reports on local retail businesses, another who covers public companies, and so forth. When soliciting coverage, it's imperative to identify which beat your story falls under, and therefore find and pitch the reporter who covers that beat. You could use a service like Bacon's or PR Newswire to figure this out, but you can also do the research at no cost by simply reading the publication or watching the broadcast you're targeting. A preliminary phone call to the newsroom, asking who covers this beat, can't hurt, either. (I actually recommend that you call even if you use one of these outside services, since members of the media are constantly changing jobs, and you don't want to send your pitch to someone who is no longer even there.)

> *Make it easy for the media to cover your business by giving them newsworthy story ideas.*

Once you identify your target, you have to give them a story that's worth telling. We thought that Build-A-Bear Workshop, in and of itself, was a legitimate story in the early days. Back then, we worked hard to tell reporters about the company and what it stood for. Our original hook was the fact that we were this brand-new retail company opening a new store in their local market. That alone was often enough to garner us some coverage. But, in some instances, we had to bait the hook with another worm.

We're well known as a good corporate citizen, and throughout the year in markets around the country we raise money for local and national causes. This topic often brings the media to our door. In addition, we are the subject of frequent human-interest stories. A lot of good things happen at our stores, and we've come to realize that these are just the kind of feel-good stories reporters like to cover—and that regular folks like to hear about.

What sorts of things am I referring to? We pitched an idea about a little girl who saved up the allowance money she earned over the summer and spent it all at our store to make animals for sick children at a local hospital. We also alerted local reporters to a story about a soldier who proposed to his girlfriend at one of our stores the day before he was deployed to Iraq. (The media covered both of these stories and countless others like them in the past eight years.)

> *Identify which reporters are likely to do a story on you, and target your carefully crafted pitches to them.*

Jill Saunders and others in our corporate PR department have worked hard to teach our associates what makes a good news story, and they're always on the lookout for those great human interest tales that spotlight what Build-A-Bear Workshop stands for and what the company means to our Guests. Our associates also understand the urgency and timely nature of these stories, and they're quick to funnel the information to the PR department so they can promptly alert the media.

Remember my fictional scenario about the not-so-new car dealership seeking media coverage? How could that business use the PR strategies outlined in this chapter? First, the owner should identify those reporters who are most likely to cover his business based on their beats and he should target his pitches to them.

Since the opening of his business is old news, perhaps he could offer himself up as a source for a story about how to shop for a used car. He could pitch a human-interest piece about a customer or employee with a compelling story to tell. He could link up with a charity and donate a few cars and cash to the cause. Or he could stage a special event, such as inviting all the town's high school honor students to register to win a free car. I bet the local media would cover any of those stories, given the right pitch and persistence.

The rules for pitching the media are similar to the rules for writing a good newspaper article.

Who? The right reporter.
What? A newsworthy story, pegged to an event or a compelling angle.
When? Timeliness is critical.
Where? Think of the local impact.
Why? Make sure there's a "so what?" factor that the reporter can't resist.

Respond to the Media

Now that you know how to get the media interested in you and your business, it's crucial to know what to do when a reporter comes calling. We all hope they'll show interest in response to a pitch we've submitted. But, in the real world, there are many reasons—some good, some bad—why a reporter may want to interview you.

There are many good and bad reasons a reporter might want to interview you.

In all cases, you should be well prepared each time an inquiry comes by having a quick, honest, thoughtful, and thorough response at the ready. It's impossible for me to list every reason a reporter might call, but here are a few possibilities:

The good:

- A reporter is intrigued by what you do and wants to write a story about your company.
- The newspaper is seeking business sources to interview for a feature on a particular topic on which you can offer perspective.
- Your business has won an award or gained some other kind of recognition that has generated media interest.

> *Always be prepared to address the media with a quick, honest, thoughtful, and thorough response.*

The bad:

- Your business has been the victim of a crime or some other disaster.
- A customer has taken a complaint about your business to the local media.
- Someone who works for your company has been accused of a crime or other wrongdoing.
- You company's stock has fallen significantly.
- Your quarterly profit and earnings didn't match your projections.

> *Set up a system for handling media calls, and have a point person who should screen all such inquiries.*

As you can imagine, this list could go on for pages, but I won't waste any more space with hypothetical scenarios. Instead, I'm going to talk about how to control your response to a media inquiry.

We have a system set up at Build-A-Bear Workshop to handle media calls. Requests for information and interviews are always filtered through our public relations department. That's important. Reporters working on a story may call any number of people in a company seeking comment. Employees should know ahead of time how to handle these requests. Specifically, are they allowed to speak to reporters without prior management approval, or should they refer the reporter to someone else? This is not the same thing as circumventing the media. Quite the contrary. It's about getting them in touch with the people who are best equipped to handle their requests and questions. Our corporate PR department coordinates all our media coverage, but our store managers and Bear Builder associates are often the ones who go on camera to talk about the company.

When a media request comes in, we ask a series of questions that help us better understand what type of information the reporter is looking for: What is your angle? Is this a feature on our company, or we part of a larger story? When will the story come out? Are you looking to interview someone? If so, what questions are you looking to get answered? What is your deadline? What other companies are you interviewing? We also "Google" reporters to see what types of stories they write and learn more about their style.

> *Never give a reporter the response, "No comment."*

Once we have those answers, we decide whether to participate in the story. We almost always say yes, even when the angle seems negative or unfavorable toward our company.

We rarely issue the all-too-common "No comment," unless it has to do with requests to comment on rumors. Now that we're a public company, we also have to be careful about what we say concerning financial performance and other business-related issues due to stringent regulations by the Securities and Exchange Commission.

> *Your relationship with the media should be based on truthfulness and mutual respect.*

That said, avoiding reporters is rarely a good strategy. The media is a great tool for getting information out to the public, be it for an event you're planning, a new product launch, sharing financial information, responding to bad news, or changing unfavorable perceptions. Besides, "No comment" often has the implied connotation, "We're guilty of something bad and don't want to discuss it," whether that's true or not.

I think many companies avoid talking to the media when there is something negative going on because they don't see how any good can come of it. However, I believe the best thing to do is come up with an honest statement based on the situation you are in. This accomplishes two things: It prevents the negative "No comment" the media will undoubtedly use if you don't respond. Second, it will improve your credibility with that reporter in the future—and also likely enhance your reputation among those consumers who read or hear that news story.

During my decades in the public eye, I've learned that most reporters are fair and accurate in their reporting and that they have long memories. You don't want to burn a bridge with a reporter by lying or obfuscating the facts. Your relationships with the media are like any others you have in business; they should be based on truthfulness and mutual respect. The reporter who calls you today on a negative story may be the same one who calls tomorrow for a positive one. Your dealings with the media should be based on straightforward communications.

> *Being uncooperative won't stop a reporter from writing a story.*

Speed and honesty are critical elements of good crisis communications. In the event of a crisis, respond quickly. Be proactive, not reactive. Share as much information as possible, and always be truthful in the statements you make to the press. It's also important to communicate your PR message throughout the company, so employees and others on the executive team understand the company's position and know which of their colleagues are the designated spokespeople on the issue.

Luckily, most of our dealings with the media begin and end positively. But we do get the occasional hardball request. A lot of times even if we know reporters are angling for a negative story, we'll still consent to an interview and might even invite them to one of our stores or World Bearquarters so they can see how we operate.

Being uncooperative won't stop reporters from writing a negative or critical article. Quite the contrary. It might motivate them to chase the story more vigorously. Communicating with a reporter at least gives you the chance to tell your side of the story in the way you want it to be told. And you just may be lucky enough the change the angle so it benefits you and casts your company in a good light. You ought to take every opportunity to turn a negative story into a positive one.

I wrote earlier about how an article in the *St. Louis Business Journal* brought Build-A-Bear Workshop to the attention of our first outside investor. When the reporter first called, I knew she was more interested in why I left my 20-year career at May Department Stores, a story I really didn't want to rehash. But I invited her to my office anyway, answered her questions honestly, and told her about this brand-new business and concept I had for revolutionizing experiential mall-based retailing. She came to the interview intending to write one story, and left with an even better one that benefited Build-A-Bear Workshop immensely. Imagine if I'd turned down that interview. It would have been like turning down millions of dollars and the opportunity for great mentors like Barry and Wayne.

Reporters are like the rest of us. Sometimes they make mistakes. If that happens in a story written about your business, by all means call the reporter, point out the error, and request a correction. Most will apologize profusely and correct the mistake at their first opportunity. Accept the apology and correction, and don't hold the mistake against the reporter if he or she calls again to do another story on your business. Your graciousness will likely strengthen your relationship and probably make the reporter more diligent about doing fact-checking in the future. He or she may also feel compelled to give you more coverage in the future to make up for the mistake. Better yet, ask whether you can fact-check the article yourself before it goes to press. Not all reporters will comply, but some will because they want an honest and accurate story, too.

> *Always be prompt when responding to media requests.*

Of course, if a reporter refuses to own up to a legitimate error, you have every right to be angry. You can inform the reporter's editor of the situation and about his or her unwillingness to make it right. If you like, you can consider that bridge burned and refuse to deal with that reporter in the future. (Even under these circumstances, this can be a precarious tactic. As you know, reporters stick to their beats. So, if you want coverage in a certain publication or on a particular newscast, you may have to suck it in and deal with that reporter anyway.)

Enough about the challenging part of dealing with the media. I'm confident that most of your dealings with reporters will be positive ones, like most of mine have been. But I wanted to arm you with all the information you need to be ready for anything that may be thrown your way.

In closing, one thing to keep in mind when dealing with reporters is that you must be prompt when responding to their inquiries. That's because all reporters—especially those working for a daily newspaper or television station—work on extremely tight deadlines. Sometimes they may have only an hour or two before a story has to be turned in for publication or broadcast. That's why you need to respond to all media inquiries immediately. As an added bonus, once they know you're good at getting back to them quickly, reporters will use you as a source more often. The first time you fail to respond promptly will almost certainly be the last time they give you a call. That's why I strongly suggest giving reporters your cell phone number if you are the primary point of contact, so they can get in touch with you wherever you go. If someone else handles your press relations, the same principle applies to them.

Above all, the easier you make a reporter's job, the more likely you are to get good coverage . . . and see your name in print to your benefit over and over again.

Advertise Smart

A s great as publicity and other forms of free media attention are, you'll likely want to supplement these efforts with at least some form of paid advertising.

It's only within the past several years that Build-A-Bear Workshop has had the national presence necessary to support a national advertising campaign, including television commercials and placements in some of the top consumer magazines for children.

In 2005, we spent close to $29 million, or about 7.5 percent of our revenues, on advertising. But not so long ago my company was in the same boat you probably find yourself in. We had a message to get out, yet limited resources to do so.

Figuring out how much to spend on paid advertising is tricky.

Figuring out how to advertise, how much to spend, and where to place your ads is a tricky proposition. It's important to start by understanding the three primary reasons companies advertise:

1. To build and sustain brand awareness. This is the reason most big companies, like Coca-Cola, General Electric (GE), and Wal-Mart, advertise.
2. To notify consumers about a new product or service—or one they are unfamiliar with.
3. To publicize an event, sale, or other promotion and attract attendance for it.

Your advertising needs probably fit into one of the first two categories, but you'll no doubt want to place some ads to help identify and establish your brand and reinforce your standing in the marketplace as well.

There are essentially three categories of advertising available to most businesses. Conventional options include newspapers, radio, television, consumer magazines, trade magazines, and billboards. You may also choose to filter your message through such new media options as e-mail blasts, search engines, and web site banner ads, where you can either pay for the impressions delivered or the number of customers who actually click on the ad. Your third advertising option is direct to consumer and includes things like direct mail.

The 7.5 percent we spent on advertising includes creative expenses (what we paid our ad agency to produce the print ads, radio spots, and television commercials) and the cost of placing the ads in the media (the rate for magazine and newspaper space and for television and radio airtime). Depending on the business, companies might budget 3 percent to 10 percent of gross sales or billings for advertising.

Determining what to spend on each campaign is trickier, as is deciding where to place your ads. In planning an advertising effort, you need to determine the goal of that campaign and how you're going to meet it. Ask these questions: Who am I trying to reach?

What's the most effective (and cost-effective) way of reaching that audience? You may need help from an independent media buyer to make those decisions.

> *When planning an advertising campaign, choose the medium that delivers the biggest audience for your business at the best price.*

The industry has several different ways of measuring a medium's efficiency. On television, it's through Nielsen ratings. In radio, it's through Arbitron ratings. Most printed publications have actual circulation figures audited by a third-party company. Ratings and circulation numbers give advertisers quantifiable information about whom their message is reaching and sometimes provide very specific demographic details about that audience. Using the available data, it is possible to determine how much it will cost to reach each customer with your advertising message. Your goal is to choose the medium that delivers the biggest audience at the best price.

Novices always consider price, but they often fail to evaluate the other side of the coin, namely a publication's or show's effectiveness in reaching the desired audience. For instance, most cities have a main newspaper and a variety of other publications, some of which are distributed for free. Generally speaking, it costs more to advertise in a publication with paid circulation than one given away for free. That makes it difficult for many start-up businesses to afford to advertise in the daily newspaper or in national consumer or trade magazines. They therefore tend to flock to other publications with cheaper page rates. But they fail to assess how effective those publications are in reaching potential customers. I'd be wary of advertising in any publication without audited circulation numbers because there's no way to independently verify that it is being read by as many people as its publisher, editors, and sales reps claim. Of course, there are times you may want to advertise in a niche publication, such as an employment guide or a local travel magazine, because that's what your customers are reading, even if audited circulation figures aren't readily available.

> *If you can't afford prime time TV ads, consider buying "fringe" spots.*

Many companies aspire to advertise on television, but TV commercials are expensive to produce and airtime is costly. You can't scrimp on your budget if you want your television campaign to be successful. You must spend money on a professional-quality production. And you'll need to buy enough spots in highly rated local, network, or cable shows that your audience watches, programming in enough frequency so they see your message repeatedly. Otherwise, the effort is a waste of time and money. If you can't afford to do an effective television campaign, spend the money on less-expensive radio instead, or take a multifaceted approach, combining print, radio, billboards, Internet, and direct-to-consumer marketing.

When your budget is limited, it pays to be savvy in your advertising choices. If you decide to advertise on television but can't afford the prime time TV slots, consider buying what's known as the "fringe," commercial spots that air just before and after prime time. They're much cheaper, yet you still have the opportunity to reach those target viewers who have tuned in early and those who leave their TVs on after their favorite shows have ended.

One strategy that was very effective for us in the beginning was taking advantage of the co-op advertising programs offered by the malls where we are located. The mall would purchase a big ad and then let merchants buy a slice of it to promote their businesses. These co-op ads delivered a big audience without a big price tag.

Another thing we did in the beginning was focus our ad dollars on acquiring new customers. To do so, we advertised in tourist publications in those cities where we had stores. We used public relations, namely story pitches to local newspapers and television stations, to spread the word further and to generate local business. Finally, we communicated directly with existing customers through e-mail and direct-marketing techniques.

> *Because the Internet is dynamic, you can tailor your online advertising efforts to fit your budget.*

The Internet is a fairly affordable place to advertise. You can use your own customer e-mail lists and send information directly to consumers. You can buy prime placement in search engines, and you can purchase banner ads on web sites that your core customers visit. Because the Internet is dynamic, you can tailor your online advertising efforts to fit your budget.

If you're starting a new company, another cost-effective strategy to consider is event sponsorship, latching onto things that already have a value for your target customers. This is essentially co-branding, tying your brand to another that resonates with the consumer you want to reach. It combines public relations, advertising, and marketing. Here's an example. Let's say an optometry practice opens a second office in a different town. Based on the location of that new office and the doctor's expertise, the practice decides to target young families as its core customers. It's located next door to a huge soccer complex where every soccer team in the county plays. The optometrist may co-brand by sponsoring a local soccer team and giving each player a goodie bag that includes a soccer ball, water bottle, and T-shirt imprinted with the practice's logo. These advertising efforts can be supplemented with billboards, newspaper advertisements, and direct mailings to families living near the office.

> *Earmark a set percentage of revenues for advertising.*

When it comes to advertising, by all means consider every option at your disposal. Earmark a set percentage of revenues for advertising and look for opportunities that allow you to effectively and inexpensively reach your target customers.

Create Buzz

As we've already discussed, buzz is the best form of advertising for any brand. You want people to always talk positively about your company—and to do it often. But how can you make that happen? In the next few pages, I'll answer that question with specific suggestions. I'll also fill you in on some of the buzz-building techniques we and other talked-about companies have used.

It's easier for a new product or company to get buzz. After all, when something exciting or different hits the market, the natural inclination among consumers is to talk about it. Diets are a perfect example. We learn that a friend or celebrity has dropped pounds using some weight-loss plan, and suddenly it's the diet everyone's on and talking about. But losing weight is harder than people think, so one new hot diet always supplants the last. Scarsdale, the Zone, Atkins, South Beach. Which one will we be buzzing about next?

Fortunately, you don't have to be a fad to get buzz. There are clever, yet honest, ways to cultivate and create buzz. And most of them are pretty easy to execute.

> *You want people to talk often about how great your company is.*

Buzz involves people seeing other people having fun and wanting to be a part of it. A buzzworthy product, like a Louis Vuitton handbag or a stay at the hip W Hotel chain, becomes a status symbol. It's the thing everyone wants, the place you want to be, the club everyone wants to join.

When creating buzz for your business, tap into those notions of popularity and exclusivity. We've found that special events, including product launches and grand openings, can really drive buzz. When we invite Guests to a VIP event, like a store opening, we always encourage them to bring two or three friends. Often, these friends are people who haven't been to a Build-A-Bear Workshop store before. If everyone we invite brings along some friends, we suddenly have a big crowd and are attracting more attention from passersby. Everyone wants to see what's going on inside, and the buzz grows.

Faced with a crowd, it's human nature to ask, "Hey, what's going on?" and to try and catch a glimpse. How many times have you been caught in a traffic jam on the highway and asked that same question, only to discover that you and other rubberneckers had caused the logjam?

> *Buzz involves people seeing others having fun at your business.*

Last year at our New York store, I was outside mingling with the hundreds of people standing in line. As I walked by, one man tugged at my sleeve and asked, "What's this all about?" He didn't even know he was waiting to go inside a Build-A-Bear Workshop store. He'd seen the line and simply wanted to be a part of the excitement that was brimming around him. That's the kind of buzz you want. (By the way, he stayed in line, went inside, and made a large purchase!)

When hosting a special event, it always helps to play up the exclusive angle and give your Guests a takeaway gift that will make them feel special and help them remember your company. At our events, we usually give everyone who walks through the door badges on lanyards that look like backstage passes. (Guests tend to wear these home, letting the badges serve as walking billboards for our stores.) We don't hand out free animals. But when people leave, we thank them with a small party favor—often a $5 gift card, a limited-edition accessory, or a small token, like a key chain, that they'll use again and again.

Product launches also offer the perfect opportunity for buzzworthy events. We always plan a special promotion around the introduction of a new animal. For years, department stores have held special events to launch new cosmetics lines or staged fashion shows to welcome a new season or designer to the assortment.

> *When creating buzz, tap into the notions of popularity and exclusivity.*

Charitable events, in addition to being a great way of doing business, also are effective ways to generate buzz. You're almost always guaranteed media coverage when you raise money or awareness for a good cause. The event will also attract like-minded people, who will be more willing to buzz about your company because you support a common cause.

Our birthday parties are another great example of how we create buzz. Some of the kids who come to parties have already been to one of our stores before, but many have not. Their first introduction to our stores is this super special event, and it increases the likelihood that they'll tell their own friends about us. What's just as common is that kids who visit the store as a party guest return on their own birthdays, bringing in yet more new Guests. In addition, when there's a party going on, it raises the energy level, and that radiates to others in the mall who pass by the store.

Birthday parties aren't just the province of kid-oriented companies. I know of many adult venues—spas, baseball parks, beading stores, beauty salons, cooking stores, and boutiques—that hold parties for their customers. They have the same opportunity to use these small gatherings to generate buzz.

> *Charitable events offer an effective way to generate buzz.*

Friends and family events involve the entire workforce in buzz cultivation. Here's how this tool, used very successfully by retailers like the Gap and Old Navy, works: Employees hand out postcards inviting their friends, relatives, and mall coworkers to a special sale, either during regular store hours or after hours. Invited guests usually get a special gift or discount, and they're made to feel part of an exclusive club. Here, the buzz is multifaceted. Employees are buzzing by inviting people to the sale, and those same guests add to the buzz by telling their friends about the special sale.

I know the company has been going through some trying times lately, but Krispy Kreme remains an exemplary buzz marketer. Its store openings are one of the greatest examples how word of mouth can help a company.

In new markets, Krispy Kreme builds anticipation for opening day to a fever pitch. Its strategies for accomplishing this are surprisingly simple. A countdown sign at the store construction site teases customers that hot doughnuts will soon be available. The company blitzes the media in the months prior to entering a market, so that by the time opening day arrives most people have already seen or read multiple times that Krispy Kreme is coming to town. These tactics alone draw crowds to the stores, but Krispy Kreme does still more to build buzz to a crescendo. The company often links its grand openings to a local charity. Scout troops and similar organizations are invited to camp out overnight in the store parking lot. In addition, Krispy Kreme gets the hottest local radio show to broadcast live from the parking lot on opening day, and it invites television reporters to do live reports that first morning. As the message that Krispy Kreme is *the* place to be reaches more people, the crowd swells and the buzz grows.

> *Utilize your existing customers to get buzz going, and plan events that no one can resist coming to.*

If you want to get people talking about your business, utilize your existing customers to get the buzz going and plan events that no one can resist coming to. In turn, you'll start hearing the din of cash registers ringing like a beautiful symphony, and know you're at the start of something big.

Use the Web Wisely

rarely issue mandates. Just ask anyone who works with me.

But here's one that I'm going to give you: Every business *must* have a web site.

> *Every business __must__ have a web site.*

In this day and age, a web site is imperative to the success of your company. Consumers worldwide have become accustomed to going to the Internet when they need information, whether it's about something happening halfway around the world or in their own neighborhood. People look up telephone numbers online. They book airline tickets and hotel rooms. When they're house hunting, they go online first to browse the photos that real estate agents have posted on their sites. They entertain themselves with online video games. They find out what movies are playing and where. They skim the menus from their favorite restaurants and figure out if, calorie-wise, they can afford a Big Mac or triple mocha with extra whip. They buy books and music—and anything else you could imagine—online. They find dates and mates. They read the news and get weather forecasts.

Businesses without a Web presence are ignoring a valuable and crucial connection point with customers. In addition, the Web is another platform to build, bolster, and promote your brand.

I started my company smack in the middle of the dot-com era, so we've had a web site from the very beginning. Soon after launching, we enabled it for e-commerce, so people could shop with us online. Having an e-commerce site, then and now, seems to be the holy grail to which companies aspire online. But it's probably the *least* important way the majority of bricks and mortar companies should use the Web. People who don't realize that miss out on the power the Internet can have on their business.

Unless you aim to be the next Amazon.com, *selling* on the Internet shouldn't be your priority. Instead, you ought to focus on building an online community that reflects your brand, offers customers vital information, and enhances your ability to communicate (and stay connected) with them.

Ronnie Gaubatz joined our company in 1999 as Master Web Bear, after having worked as a consultant and Web developer for other companies for many years. Much of what you'll read in this chapter I learned from her.

> *Companies without a Web presence are ignoring a valuable and crucial connection point with customers.*

Setting up a web site doesn't have to be expensive. In my business plan, I earmarked $50,000 in marketing dollars for the web site and hired professional developers to complete the job. If you run a small business, you should be able to build your own site using the various templates and tools available through most Internet service providers for a fraction of that cost. As your company grows, you can funnel more profits into improving your site.

As I said earlier, we didn't build our web site to rack up sales online (although it is very successful). Instead, we like to use it to increase business at our stores. The number one goal of our site is to drive traffic to our physical locations because we know that's where our associates can deliver on the brand promise.

How do we do this? We give Guests fun things to do while at our web site, and tempt them with calendar listings and other details about what's going on in our stores.

I think we've made our web site dynamic and a fun place to hang out, mimicking online, as best we can, the experience we deliver every day in our stores. The web site certainly is not meant to be a substitute for our stores, but we strive to keep it fresh and exciting and packed with information that our Guests need. We're constantly running online promotions and contests, which we publicize on our store receipts, Cub Condo carrying cases, and shopping bags, and in advertisements. And we've created games and other fun things, such as screen savers and printable party invitations, that lure visitors back to the site, and therefore to our stores, often.

The average visitor to our web site spends 16 minutes there playing games, shopping for accessories for their animals, browsing our online catalog, and simply exploring. That's an incredible statistic. As Ronnie told me, "In my previous life if I could get people to come to a web site that I developed and spend two minutes there, I would do a backflip."

Selling *on the Internet shouldn't be your priority. Instead, focus on building an online community that enhances your ability to* communicate *with customers*.

Even if you don't match our 16 minutes, you can maximize your web site to acquire new and repeat customers. If you set your sights higher, you can create a web site that your customers will find valuable enough to spend their time on.

At the very least, your web site should contain basic information about your business: what you do, where you're located, your telephone number, and other contact information.

But I really think you ought to strive to provide more by creating a community where customers can come for information, fun, and maybe even deals.

Lots of companies offer coupons through their web sites or send out special e-mail offers. That gives people a reason to come to both your web site *and* your place of business. It's what I call using the Web wisely.

Blogging is also an increasingly important and popular tool. Some advertising agencies use Weblogs, or blogs, to keep clients abreast of trends in the industry. Newspapers are embracing blogs as a tool to deliver information to readers more quickly and to compete with other media. Blogging is applicable to so many companies. Wouldn't you love it if your doctor wrote a blog with advice on how to prevent a cold or when to schedule an appointment so you wouldn't have to wait?

Stonyfield Farms, which produces yogurt and other organic dairy products, employs a corporate blogger and maintains four separate regularly updated blogs where customers can find out information, as well as interact with Stonyfield staff members and other customers. One blog includes dispatches from one of the company's organic farm suppliers. The others provide news about women's health, information for parents of babies, and editorial comments about nutrition in schools.

Fun and games help drive the traffic at our web site, but other businesses could benefit from becoming a resource for helpful information. L. L. Bean offers a plethora of useful information in a section of its web site called "Explore the Outdoors." The site offers primers on popular outdoor sports, suggestions on where to participate in these activities, maps of the Appalachian Trail, conservation lessons, and links to other useful web sites, including the Weather Channel and the Outdoor Life Network.

> *Unless you have only an online presence, the number one goal of your site should be to drive business to your physical locations, where you can deliver on your brand promise.*

Why not turn your web site into an information resource for your customers, as well as an advertising tool for your brand? For example, a dry cleaner could post weekly tips on stain removal. A health club could offer healthy recipes and diet and exercise logs. A moving company could link to the United States Postal Service's online change-of-address form, offer packing tips, and provide a tool to help figure out how many boxes and rolls of bubble wrap you'll need. A movie theater ought to offer reviews, movie trivia, quizzes, and perhaps even some celebrity gossip.

As you forge your company's online identity, your first step is registering your Web address or domain name through one of the many sites that make this process a breeze. Avoid domain squatters—people who buy up Web addresses and try to resell them for a profit. In addition, you may want to register variations of your company name, so that if someone misspells it, abbreviates it, or adds punctuation, they'll still find you. (For example, customers of The Bombay Company can find the retailer on the Web at www.bombaycompany.com, www.bombayco.com, and www.the bombaycompany.com.)

Then, decide on what sort of content and features you want to include. If you lack the skills or time to build the site yourself, bring in outsiders to help. You can hire a Web developer or contract with an outside firm, as we did when resources were tight. Whether you hire an employee or a contractor, make sure they understand your vision for the site. You'll want to find someone who realizes that a web site is an ongoing project, something that is never finished.

> *Keep your site exciting and packed with information customers need.*

A big mistake lots of companies make is launching their web sites too early, before they have created enough content. Worse yet, they'll post a message that says, "Under Construction" and leave it there for aeons. You want your online address to be a place where people come for information about your business. Companies can drive customers away with their useless, uninformative, lackluster sites. They're certainly not giving customers a reason to visit them online again.

If your web site isn't ready when you open your doors, I suggest doing one of two things. Either delay publicizing your web site or create a teaser or countdown page that says something like "Coming in 10 Days." That gives your customers an incentive to return. Just make sure that when they do, the payoff is worth the wait.

If you spend the time to build a good web site, you must make a commitment to maintain it and, most importantly, keep the content fresh and up to date. Sure, this takes a commitment of time and resources, but it's definitely worth it. There's nothing Web surfers hate more than logging onto a site and discovering outdated content, like a home page that hasn't been changed in two years, or a calendar that is stuck three months in the past. In addition to being a whiz at Web design and marketing, Ronnie also has a way with words. She says logging on to an outdated site is like "biting on a piece of aluminum foil." Ouch!

Content, like bread, gets stale. Never forget that. Every business has a threshold for what's old. In our case, the web site changes somewhat every day. You must identify when your content gets old and develop systems for updating it. I'm not a Web programmer, but it's fairly easy to update a web site regularly using automated processes. Automation and the use of standardized templates are two ways we're able to manage our own site at Build-A-Bear Workshop. Our Web staff is relatively small—just Ronnie and three creative developers. Many people are surprised when I tell them we have only four people on the team because we have such a large, dynamic site.

> *Register several domain name variations of your company name so customers can easily find you.*

One last lesson on web sites, and it's one you've learned elsewhere in the book: Create your web site with your core customer in mind. That may mean limiting the bells and whistles.

Our web site, www.buildabear.com, has a lot of nifty features, and our designers use animation (namely, Macromedia Flash) to bring it to life. But we're always very careful not to overdesign the site or use technology that the average computer and Internet connection can't handle. You shouldn't require your online visitors to download software to view or use your web site; that is like charging them an admission fee to shop in your store.

We've built our web site around the capabilities of an entry-level computer that someone might buy from their local store for $599. (These machines are likely to include Adobe Acrobat Reader software and come with Web browsers than can handle Flash animations.) We once had to be more careful about including features that required a lot of bandwidth. But as high-speed Internet connections have proliferated, this has become less of a concern.

In business, a web site has become as essential as a telephone. Develop and use your site wisely, and you'll gain a valuable tool for promoting your brand.

Embrace Viral Marketing

Psst. I've got to tell you about this great new tool for creating excitement about your business. The folks at the ad agencies call it viral marketing. That's a fancy term for word-of-mouth advertising delivered on the Web or through e-mail messages, then passed along by your customers to their friends. Some clever writers have christened it word-of-mouse. Whatever you call it, it sure is effective. Be sure to pass it on.

> *The Internet has created new opportunities for companies to communicate with and market to their customers.*

The Internet has created new opportunities for companies to communicate with and market to their customers. One of the best of these is viral marketing. As the name implies, it's a way of spreading your message from one person to another—the same way a virus spreads. We've found it to be an efficient and fairly inexpensive way to enlist our loyal customers to create buzz for the company.

Hotmail was one of the first companies to use viral marketing to promote its free e-mail service. Anytime a Hotmail user sends an e-mail, the company attaches a promotional tagline and Web link to the bottom of the message. In the beginning, Hotmail used this line to promote its own service. That proved incredibly successful. Within the first 18 months, Hotmail had signed up 12 million subscribers on a marketing budget of less than $500,000. Microsoft now owns Hotmail, and uses the tagline to promote its other products and services.

> *Viral marketing is a way to spread your message from one person to another online—the same way a virus spreads.*

The Hotmail campaign was so successful because the referral to try the service came from the recipients' friends, family members, and coworkers—people they trusted. That's the crux of viral marketing—spreading the word through a series of trustworthy referrals. It's the complete opposite of spam because the e-mail comes from someone the recipient knows, not an unwelcome third party.

At Build-A-Bear Workshop, we use multiple forms of viral marketing. Whenever customers receive an e-mail announcement or newsletter from us, they have the option of clicking on a button to "Send to a Friend." In our Web store, we use the same tool as many other online retailers. Shoppers may send a friend an e-mail link to the item. Our electronic HoneyCards are another clever way we entice people to tell others about our brand. Anyone who receives one of the online greeting cards has the opportunity to pass that message along to someone else or personalize their own HoneyCard. Either option helps fuel the buzz.

Recently, we ran a contest that enlisted our Guests' help in designing a new outfit for Pawlette Coufur, our fashion mascot. At the contest Web page, we included lots of games and quizzes that our customers could send to their friends. That was one of our most successful contests—we received more than 6,000 entries—because it spread virally. (Some Web surfers even blogged about it.) By the way, this was 6,000 very detailed designs, not just entry blanks. For these types of interactive activities, our entries number in the hundreds of thousands.

> *Spreading the word through a series of trustworthy referrals is the crux of viral marketing.*

There's really no limit to what you can do with viral marketing. Our approach has been relatively simple. But other businesses have created entire web sites specifically for the purpose of marketing a message virally.

In April 2004, Burger King and its ad agency created a buzzworthy web site at www.subservientchicken.com. On the site, an actor in a chicken suit responds to typed commands: dance, sit, cluck—whatever visitors dream up. Tens of millions have visited the site and forwarded the link to their friends, helping to spread the word about Burger King's new TenderCrisp sandwiches. The message in those millions of e-mails—"Finally somebody in a chicken costume who will do whatever you want"—closely parallels the tagline for the sandwiches: "Chicken just the way you want it."

In lieu of traditional television advertising, Unilever created a series of animated Web soap operas in 2005, called Webisodes, to promote its I Can't Believe It's Not Butter! spray. Unilever customers received an e-mail inviting them to tune in to the short, campy soaps online. Once they watched, they were enticed to spread the word:

"Go ahead . . . tell your friends! Who said gossip was a bad thing? Let your friends know that something big is happening in the refrigerator!" Clever, indeed. We're even considering producing something similar for Build-A-Bear Workshop.

Perhaps the best example ever of viral marketing is the hit movie, *The Blair Witch Project*. In advance of its theatrical release, producers created a web site that introduced the world to the three college students who reportedly disappeared in the woods of Burkittsville, Maryland, while shooting a documentary.

The site included all kinds of spooky details about the legend of the Blair witch, as well as a journal, photographs, and video clips of the "lost" filmmakers during their final days in the woods. In addition, the producers put up "missing" posters at the Cannes Film Festival.

> *There is really no limit to what you can do with viral marketing.*

The movie, supposedly a documentary comprised of footage discovered in the woods, promised to explore the mystery of what happened to the college students. Even before the movie hit theaters, the story caught the attention of people worldwide, who perpetuated it like the urban myth that it was. Fooled by the clever marketing campaign, many believed that the trio in the movie had actually disappeared. In reality, they were actors.

Regardless, moviegoers told their friends the horrible tale of the three young people who disappeared while searching for the Blair witch. This translated into huge audiences for the movie. *The Blair Witch Project*, which cost about $25,000 to produce, grossed more than $150 million, making it the most profitable motion picture of all time.

> *If you have a database of customer e-mail addresses—and you should—orchestrate opportunities for these customers to tell their friends about your business.*

I hope these examples give you the impetus to utilize viral marketing in your own business. If you have a database of customer e-mail addresses—and you should—orchestrate opportunities for these customers to tell their friends about your business. People you reach through this method are highly likely to try your product or service because it has been referred to them by someone they trust.

Part Six

Growing Your
Business

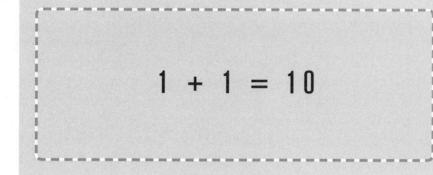

$$1 + 1 = 10$$

When it comes to business, I'm convinced it's possible to make $1 + 1 = 10$.

Unfortunately, one plus one only equals two for most companies. That's because they often try to go it alone by taking small steps, rather than seeking huge-leap strategic synergies. Sure, such moves may require sharing a cut of the profits. But when you add one great company with another, the results can be amazing.

The same thing is true when it comes to your employees. When you combine their valuable input and contributions with your own, it's like having multiple brainpower to the 10th degree.

To get through all of the loud marketing messages consumers are inundated with, your offering must be really special.

In today's world, you have to make 1 + 1 = 10—or even more. That's because consumers are inundated with loud marketing messages practically everywhere they turn. As a result, in order to get through all of this noise, your offering has to be really special. One way to accomplish this is by adding value through forming partnerships that create huge "wow" experiences for your customers.

It starts by not being afraid to seek the right strategic fits, even when the target you desire a relationship with appears to be much larger and seemingly unapproachable. For instance, several years ago I observed that many of our Guests also shopped at Limited Too, a fashion store catering to young girls. Given how popular the chain's clothes were, I thought it would be neat if we could offer Limited Too outfits for our bears. At the time, we were just a $200 million company, dwarfed by Limited Too's $600 million in annual sales. But I knew we had a lot to offer and was convinced that by pooling our resources together, we would make 1 + 1 = 10 for both of us. The company ultimately agreed, and sales of our Limited Too wear for bears have exceeded even our most optimistic projections.

Another 10 on our wow scale came when we approached Major League Baseball about offering licensed uniforms for our bears. Some might wonder what stuffed animals have to do with a nine-inning game played by a bunch of tough guys. Actually, I've found that putting together two seemingly divergent ideas can create some of the biggest connections for your customers. Indeed, our licensed baseball uniform bears are now among our most popular, attracting interest from both sexes of all ages. As a matter of fact, we now have our own stores at several major league ballparks. Who would have thought this partnership could be so strong?

> *Don't be afraid to seek the right strategic fits, even if the target you desire seems unapproachable.*

We've formed similar 1 + 1 = 10 alliances with the National Basketball Association, the National Football League, Disney, Warner Brothers, Skechers Footwear, and even the Macy's Thanksgiving Day Parade, which has featured a Build-A-Bear Workshop float in its lineup for the past four years. These partnerships give us exposure to audiences and markets we could never reach on our own, and vice versa. And every year the list gets longer.

The same holds true when it comes to your employees. Whenever you put teams of bright workers together with a common goal and ask them to join forces, they can quickly take a concept that might seem complicated or less obvious and turn it into something fantastic (not to mention profitable). Since our associates are always on the front lines, I make sure to involve them in a variety of different projects throughout the company. As a result, every single accomplishment of major significance in our history has been largely a consequence of their collective input and involvement—from our decision to go into the party business to the opening of our biggest store in the world in New York City.

> *Putting two seemingly divergent ideas together can create some of the biggest connections for your customers.*

The formation of "friends 2B made," our companion doll making business, is a good illustration of this process in action. The idea to start a doll store sifted in my head for several years, though I never put the wheels in motion. Then I decided to sit down with a group of 10 Build-A-Bear Workshop associates from various locations around the country. I brought them to our World Bearquarters for two days and brainstormed about the concept and how we could develop it into something that would create an exciting, but different, experience from our core stores.

The input from these associates was invaluable, and much of it was learned from working with and listening to our Guests. After gathering all of this feedback, we put a plan together and launched our first "friends 2B made" store about six months later. It has been a successful concept that is growing at a rapid pace. At the same time, this brainstorming session gave us insights into various ways to improve our core Build-A-Bear Workshop business even further.

What's more, the input from these associates changed my thinking about how to approach the concept of starting a doll store. The end result, therefore, was much different—and better—than what I would have come up with on my own.

Keep in mind that 1 + 1 = 10 doesn't have to be a multimillion dollar deal. The most important criterion is that it must be a huge win for your customers. Otherwise, the partnership will never truly be mutually beneficial. It's all about working together to create bigger and better products and services than you could on your own.

Even Disney realized that 1 + 1 = 10 when it partnered with Pixar Animation Studios to create *Toy Story* in 1995. As a result of this synergy, *Toy Story* became one of the most successful movies (animated or otherwise) in history. Even though Disney knew how to make cartoons, it didn't have expertise in the computer-generated animation Pixar has mastered. At the same time, Pixar didn't have a distribution channel or expertise for getting its films into theaters. By joining forces with the much bigger Disney, Pixar instantly became a major player in the motion picture business. The two companies subsequently produced several other movies together, including *Monsters, Inc.*, *Toy Story 2*, *Finding Nemo*, *A Bug's Life*, and *The Incredibles*—all of which were huge blockbusters.

> *Partnerships are all about working together to create something bigger and better than you could on your own.*

As you read this, you might be thinking to yourself, "This sounds great, Maxine, but I'm just a small player. How can I possibly convince a larger company to join forces with me?" The answer begins by believing you are bigger than you really are. Although I stand only four feet eleven, I feel like I'm at least seven feet tall. My favorite animal is the giraffe, and I've always tried to live up to that stature, in both my personal and my business life. Because we're a pretty high-profile company and have some big partners, a lot of people think Build-A-Bear Workshop is bigger than it is.

A photographer recently took my picture for an article in the October 2005 issue of *Fast Company* magazine. During the shoot, he commented, "I've been hearing about you for years. How many stores do you have? Like 600?" If you want to see how happy that question made me, just check out the smile on my face in the photograph that ran with the article.

In my mind, you're as big as you think you are. With that confidence in mind, come up with a precise written plan about what you want to do and why the synergy makes good sense for both sides. Make the presentation to your potential partner clear and simple, and ensure that the benefits immediately come to life. You must also demonstrate what you are willing to put on the table in order to make the deal happen, which likely means investing some of your own time and money.

> *The smaller you are, the bigger you need to look.*

I've never been one for style over substance, but I've found that when you're pitching an idea to a potential partner that is bigger than you are, you have to impress. That means looking, acting, and talking the part. In fact, the smaller you are, the bigger you need to look. When we pitched World Wildlife Fund on the idea of selling Beary Limited edition stuffed animals to help protect endangered species, we had fewer than 25 stores. Nevertheless, our presentation was perfectly polished. We went in well organized, with our talking points planned out and professional-looking handouts and props in hand. We didn't want to provide them with an easy excuse for turning us down.

It's always important to find the right person to pitch your idea to. In today's world, that's fairly easy to do. With a few Google searches, you can quickly come up with not only the correct contact with whom to speak, but also that person's telephone number and e-mail address.

Remember, just because you think it's a good idea doesn't mean everyone else will—at least not right away. You may have to knock on more than one door and refine your thinking a bit along the way before finding the right connection. But it's worth the effort, and it's the only way I know to turn simple addition into a major multiplication of success.

Live in the Now . . . and the Future

always have some sort of to-do list that I'm working on. But mine isn't just your typical random inventory of what needs to be done at the office. Ever since I was a kid, I've always written down my various goals and tracked my progress at reaching them step-by-step. It's my way of making sure that what I'm doing today will help get me where I want to be in the future.

> *Live in the now, but with a watchful eye on the future.*

That's the way I live both my personal and my business life—in the now, but with an ever-watchful eye to the future. This is a method of thinking and acting strategically without neglecting the day-to-day needs of your business.

How do I do it? I'm lucky to have a competent staff running my daily business. That gives me time to think strategically about how to map our company's future. However, without an underlying plan, there would be nothing to map. Among other things, your business plan is your company's ultimate to-do list. It is, after all, a detailed accounting of the goals you have set for yourself and your business, including a specific list of steps for getting there. Mine keeps me constantly grounded even after all of these years.

What does living now and in the future really mean? I can best explain this philosophy by telling you what *not* to do.

Don't use my advice about living in the future as an excuse to procrastinate. If there's a task that needs to be done today, don't put it off to daydream about the future. Otherwise, there may be no future at all. In year 2 of my business, I was aware of and working toward my goal for year 10, revising it accordingly as I saw how Build-A-Bear Workshop was received by the market. But my immediate actions were focused on the now, meaning the coming 24 to 36 months.

> *Pace your hiring and capital expenditures to match projected needs.*

When we had just two stores, I didn't waste money then hiring people for that point in the future when we'd have 200 stores. We paced our hiring and capital expenditures to match our projected needs. We hire and spend in advance of those needs, usually about a year out, but not so far that we squeeze our profit margins. For instance, you wouldn't want to build a new manufacturing facility if it wasn't necessary to ramp up production for another five years. It's important not to get too far ahead of yourself or customer demand.

The flip side, however, is getting so bogged down in today's projects and problems that you miss out on future opportunities. I'll admit to procrastinating in my personal life. But in business, I'm pretty proactive. It is so important to think strategically and give yourself time to execute all of your great ideas.

> *Spend in advance of your needs, but no so far out that profit margins get squeezed.*

In case you don't know the origin of the teddy bear, I'll preface my next example with a short history lesson. In 1902, President Theodore Roosevelt was on a hunting trip in Mississippi. He wasn't having much luck, so one of his buddies tied a bear cub to a tree to help him bag a kill. Roosevelt, who liked hunting for the sport and not the kill, refused to shoot the helpless, trussed animal. The tale of his compassion spread quickly. Not long after, Clifford Berryman drew a cartoon based on Roosevelt's kind act. A Brooklyn shopkeeper saw the cartoon and began selling stuffed bears, dubbed "Teddy's Bear," in his stores.

In 2002, we celebrated the 100th anniversary of the teddy bear in a major way, with special promotions in our stores, the opening of our 100th store at Roosevelt Field, and the first appearance of a Build-A-Bear Workshop float in the Macy's Thanksgiving Day Parade. We wanted to position our company as the ultimate authority on teddy bears. To accomplish this monumental task, we began well in advance of the actual event—three years, in fact—mapping out our strategy and detailing our specific promotions. Without this eye on the future, we would have missed a tremendous marketing and branding opportunity. It would not have been possible for us to open the Roosevelt Field store without ample planning, and you can't get a slot in the Macy's Thanksgiving Day Parade on short notice.

So many people miss out on opportunities in their personal and professional lives because they're not preparing for or paying attention to the future. (How many times have you been forced to turn down an invitation because you let work pile up and couldn't spare the extra hours?) Plus, when you don't prepare in advance, you often cause yourself more work and hassles in the future. I've seen that happen in our own company. I was in a store one morning and noticed that not all of the merchandise bins and clothing pegs were full.

I knew the inventory wasn't sold out. The associates simply hadn't taken time to replenish the supply from the stockroom. Every night before closing, our associates are supposed to restock our stores so they're "grand opening" ready for Guests the next morning. This particular store manager let the night shift go home early, leaving that job to the opening crew. Unfortunately, they didn't have time to get it done before the store opened, and certainly not once Guests started showing up. So, the bins stayed empty much of the day and Guests didn't get the best impression of Build-A-Bear Workshop at that location. That manager needed to start living in both the now and the future.

> *Many miss out on opportunities by not preparing for the future.*

Here's the lesson I hope you'll take away from this chapter: Be present in your decisions and actions today, but keep working toward a bigger vision. By working hard today, right now, you'll be on your way to accomplishing all of your future goals.

Learn from the Experiences of Others

Life is my graduate school.

Though I've been out of college for years, I've made the world my classroom. I try to learn something from every person I meet, every place I visit, every store I shop at, and every book I read. While fulfilling my own natural curiosity, I'm also building a tremendous idea file, based on the experiences and insights of others that I can review when I need inspiration for my own business.

Try to learn something from every person you meet, every place you visit, every book you read.

My parents, especially my mother, helped me to develop this trait. We never had much money growing up, but Mom and Dad always found a way to afford a set of *The World Book Encyclopedia* and the annual yearbook that came with it. I was a pretty inquisitive child, always interrupting my mother with lots of whys and hows. I can't remember her ever getting exasperated by my curiosity or passing off my questions as insignificant. Of course, she wouldn't always answer my questions. Instead, she encouraged me to find the answer myself, directing me to the leather-bound encyclopedia volumes.

What that taught me was to always keep my eyes open for new lessons and to seek out answers for myself. I still do that. I'm constantly seeking out lessons in everything I do, hear, and see.

I'm just as inquisitive now as when I was a child. I'm always asking people questions because I think that's one of the best ways to learn.

When I was a department store buyer, I constantly asked my vendors for their advice and input. I still do.

Very early in my career, I remember waiting to talk with a hosiery manufacturer. He was meeting with a buyer from another store, and I overheard their conversation. I thought the buyer must have been this very mature, experienced woman because she never once asked a question. Instead, she spoke very authoritatively and told the manufacturer exactly what he needed to do. When that buyer stood up to leave, I was surprised because she was young, just like me. There was no way she could possibly have known everything she seemed to.

> *One of the best ways to learn is by asking lots of questions.*

When I met with that same manufacturer, I knew I didn't know everything. I asked for his opinion on the best way to present his product in our stores. I quizzed him about packaging.

When you buy from vendors, you're buying their expertise as well as their products. So, I always listen to the insights of these vendors, knowing they can help me do my job better.

Guess what else helps in this process? Shopping! I love to shop, and I head to the mall quite often for fun. But I also shop for new ideas by noting what other retailers do right—and wrong.

Recently I was at a store searching for some khaki pants to wear as part of my Build-A-Bear Workshop uniform. I found the pants I wanted in one store, but they didn't have my correct size.

I asked the clerk whether she could order them for me. She suggested I'd have better luck ordering the pants online because they'd arrive quicker. I was certainly willing to do that, but needed the style number and asked if she could write it down—that way I'd be sure to get the same exact pair. "Sure, in a minute," the clerk replied with little enthusiasm. She never did come back to help. As a result, I walked out and bought my pants elsewhere. You can rest assured I have no plans to go back to that store anytime soon. It's amazing how one bad apple can damage your business.

I feel sorry for the company she worked for, not because it lost me as a customer, but because this woman obviously doesn't like her job very much, nor does she care about helping customers. Maybe she was indifferent because she or her store wouldn't get a commission for the online sale.

Whatever the case, every store needs to have a little form ready at the cash register just for these types of requests. It should contain a space for a description of the item and the product number. That would make it so much easier for store employees to give out valuable information that leads to additional sales.

> *When you buy from a vendor, you're also buying their expertise and insights.*

Some stores, like Chico's, bend over backwards to help customers find what they need. If your local Chico's doesn't have the item you're looking for, sales clerks will search the inventory nationwide to find it in another store and then ship the merchandise directly to you. The manager of the other Chico's store will generally even write you a personalized thank-you note. Now, that's the kind of service every retailer should emulate.

You wouldn't believe all the things I've learned from other people and businesses. You never know where—or when—inspiration will hit you.

There's a taxi driver in Chicago who absolutely stands out in the crowd. I've been lucky enough to catch a ride from him twice. When you get in his cab, he offers you a bottle of water—either ice-cold or room temperature, depending on your preference. If you're traveling with children, he'll give you a book about things to do with kids in Chicago. I think he's absolutely brilliant, and I've learned a lot from him about how a little extra effort can really wow your customers. Wouldn't you want to take a ride with him, compared to all of the other drivers with bad attitudes and dirty cars? He makes you look forward to catching a cab.

You know what else I took away from my ride with him? An idea for our business cards. This driver tacks the cards from each of his fares to the ceiling of the cab. I wanted our business cards for Build-A-Bear Workshop to be colorful and unique, not run-of-the-mill. I got lots of ideas from the cards in his cab, including the one to make the back side solid yellow instead of plain white like everyone else.

A few years ago, I had a meeting with some executives from Procter & Gamble. They were talking about some new products the company had on the horizon and how they involved consumers in the product development process.

> *Inspiration is all around you.*

One thing researchers did was tour around to state fairs and festivals with these portable bathrooms. They made sure the bathrooms, which were sponsored by the Charmin brand of toilet tissue and warmly referred to internally as "Potty Paloozas," were really clean and fresh smelling. Procter & Gamble stocked them with both famous favorites and new products it was trying to bring to market.

People lined up to use these fancy, very clean portable bathrooms, along with all the Procter & Gamble products inside. They left with a good feeling and a desire to use more of these bathroom items in their own homes.

As the executives told me about this successful promotion, my brain was going click, click, click. That's how I got the idea of developing Build-A-Bear Workshop On Tour, a store within a 53-foot tractor trailer that travels to festivals and fairs around the country. If it's good enough for Charmin, it's good enough for us.

> *Let good ideas inspire you, instead of just stealing them as your own.*

There's inspiration all around you, though most don't see it. When many hear a good idea, they slap their heads and say, "Why didn't I think of that?" Or they simply turn into copycats. That's not the right way to go about it. Learn from what others have done successfully. But let their good ideas inspire you, instead of just stealing them as your own.

Grow Without Compromise

Even if your business has yet to get off the ground, I'm sure you have extraordinary plans for it. You're probably already dreaming about how much money you'll make and how big the business will ultimately become.

Don't grow your company just for growth's sake.

As you know, I harbored those same kinds of thoughts when I made the switch from employee to entrepreneur. I knew from the very beginning that I wanted more than a single retail store. I envisioned Build-A-Bear Workshop as the multi-unit chain it has become.

As president of Payless ShoeSource, a chain with more than 4,000 stores, I was pretty familiar with many of the malls across the United States. But with the help of our real estate partner, Hycel Properties Company, I identified all the malls in the country that I wanted a presence in. Together, we set criteria for where we wanted our stores to be located in each of these properties—specifically, at the center court near other retailers for kids like Limited Too and The Children's Place.

We're still not in all of those malls yet. Sometimes spaces become available, yet we pass because the locations aren't right for us. We've turned down locations at rents that were quite low. But we don't want to grow just for growth's sake. We're not interested in watching our store count tick up, regardless of location or cost. We want to expand smartly and to grow according to plan without compromising those things that are important to our business, our brand, and our Guests.

> *Expand smartly and without compromising those things that are important to your business.*

Every entrepreneur should have a similar growth plan. You need a clear idea of when and where the company will expand, at what pace, and how. Your goal should be to make the company stronger with each expansion. If you can't make your second location as good as your first—or better—why even open it?

Of course, successful companies are often pressured to grow very quickly—and sometimes imprudently. This pressure can come from many sources: Landlords that want to make you a deal on space. Customers seeking more locations from which they can buy products and services from you. Suppliers that want a bigger slice of your business. Venture capitalists looking for a quick return on their money. Stockholders demanding a certain level of growth.

> *Your goal should be to make the company stronger with each expansion.*

When it comes to growth, you need to trust your gut. Undertake an expansion only when you're financially, operationally, and mentally prepared to do so. And grow on your own terms, according to what makes the most logical sense for you and your business.

In our case, we have very deliberately chosen to build stores in those regions that best match our core Guest demographic. We're very choosy about store locations within those markets. We will open only in the best malls and in what we consider to be prime locations within those malls. We're also attracted to malls with low vacancy rates and where the landlords are investing in the property.

> *Expand only when you're financially, operationally, and mentally prepared to do so.*

We won't compromise on those requirements. Why? Because compromising on our expansion strategy would be like compromising on sales and profits, a trade I'm unwilling to make.

In addition to all the other factors that make it a great company, I think Build-A-Bear Workshop's measured growth strategy has played a role in our tremendous success. When we move into a mall, we expect that location to deliver a certain amount of traffic, sales, and profitability—and we'll quickly nix those locations that can't support these numbers. As a result, we recoup our investment in a store in about a year, compared to the industry standard of about two years.

> *Having a bad location is a primary reason companies fail.*

Sometimes entrepreneurs fail to adequately research the local real estate market. They'll settle for space with the lowest rent without considering how much traffic it will deliver. Having a bad location is a primary reason that many companies fail. It's always prudent to choose a location that is accessible to employees and with ready access to a strong talent pool. Another factor to consider when selecting your location is its proximity to your suppliers and customers, as well as the local transportation infrastructure.

Growth doesn't always have to involve opening a new location. Sometimes companies grow through acquisition or by expanding into other areas of production. Expansion should always be a good thing; it must add to your sales and success, not rob you of these things. That's why it's important to avoid any new project that takes you away from your core business.

As you know by now, I've recently added a second experiential retail concept to our portfolio. At "friends 2B made," our Guests create their own dolls with personality. The process is very similar to Build-A-Bear Workshop. What makes "friends 2B made" such a great fit for our company is that it remains true to our core business, which is making kids happy through the process of creating their own stuffed best friends.

Never let a new project take you away from your core business.

Remember that growth for growth's sake alone is not wise. Expand your business according to your own terms and principles. The goal of growth is for you to get *better*, not just bigger.

Be Prepared for the Unimaginable

Wendy Matherne is the district manager (or Bearitory Leader) for an area that includes our store in Metairie, Louisiana, near New Orleans. When Hurricane Katrina hit the Gulf Coast in the summer of 2005, Wendy was as prepared as anyone could be in the face of a natural disaster.

Having a well-devised plan will help you to weather any crisis.

As the storm bore down on her hometown, Wendy scrambled to evacuate her own family and gather up a few of her most precious personal belongings. As she tended to this personal crisis, she also prepared for the impact Katrina would have on our store and her associates.

Knowing that Hurricane Katrina would force people to take refuge at shelters, hotels, and relatives' homes, Wendy collected cell phone and family contact numbers from every store associate. She also made sure they all knew how to reach her via cell phone and by e-mail on her BlackBerry. In addition, she set up a phone tree, assigning associates to call and check on one another's safety after the storm.

When Katrina finally hit, with more devastating force than anyone ever imagined, Wendy and the rest of the associates at the Lakeside Shopping Center Build-A-Bear Workshop store were prepared. In the aftermath, she was quickly able to locate each of her associates by telephone and find out what assistance they needed. She might well have been the one island of calm in a storm of chaos.

> *A crisis can strike at any time, and often without warning.*

Wendy's story is the ultimate example of why a crisis response plan is so important. She was prepared for the unimaginable—in this case a destructive hurricane and its chaotic aftermath. She had a well-devised plan that helped her associates weather the devastating crisis and helped us help them.

Such an incident can strike your business at any time, and often without warning. Disaster can come in many forms—a hurricane, fire, robbery, product recall, strike, negative publicity, building collapse, and so forth. You can't predict the unimaginable, but you can prepare for it, as Wendy did so effectively.

> *The best businesses are like the scouts—always prepared for anything.*

I previously mentioned that the roof caved in at the warehouse where we stored all of our merchandise during our first year in business. Our offices were on the lower level, and the upper stories of the building collapsed, destroying every teddy bear, outfit, and Cub Condo we had.

In all my musings about what could go wrong, I never imagined that would happen. Luckily, we had anticipated that *something* might go wrong in the course of business, and had a crisis response plan in place, just in case.

The warehouse manager knew whom to call when that accident happened, and I had a plan for notifying our vendors and asking them to rush out orders for replacement products. (Thankfully, we also had good relationships with each of those vendors, and they opened up their plants on the weekend to fill our orders without demanding up-front payments.)

In some cases, as with a hurricane, you may get advance warning that disaster is about to strike. Normally, however, it's impossible to predict such things. Therefore, the best businesses are like scouts—always prepared for anything. They have written contingency and crisis plans in place addressing a wide variety of potential scenarios.

> *Have a written contingency and crisis plan in place addressing a wide variety of potential scenarios.*

At Build-A-Bear Workshop, we have a number of crisis plans, some of which we've had to implement, and others that we thankfully haven't. We have plans for dealing with store electrical problems, computer system failures, breakdowns in our distribution system, natural disasters, store fires, and many other potential problems.

You'll need to tailor your crisis plans to your particular business. But there are some key steps to follow when preparing for the unimaginable.

- Put your plans in writing and make them as detailed as possible. Be sure to include checklists and important telephone numbers.
- Make certain all employees are aware that these plans exist and know how to access and implement them in an emergency.
- Plan for alternate methods of communication, such as landline telephones, two-way radios, cell phones, and e-mail.
- The focus of the plan should be on employee safety and getting your business up and running again as quickly as possible.
- Plan for contingencies and offer multiple solutions for problems.
- Designate a specific person to lead the crisis response effort.
- Set up a method—such as a phone tree, special web site, or telephone hotline—for communicating with employees, vendors, and others who are involved in the crisis.
- Determine who will deal with media inquiries and how they will be handled.

In my mind, good crisis management is rooted in effective communications and advance preparation. Planning ahead is really the key to being prepared for the unimaginable.

Innovate Incessantly

Necessity may be the mother of invention, but innovation is the engine that drives a successful business. To remain competitive and relevant to customers, companies must constantly reinvent themselves by introducing new products and improving operations.

Success can often be a barrier to change.

Success can often be a barrier to change. When a company is doing well—making money and running flawlessly—the natural tendency is to simply maintain the status quo. No one wants to upset the apple cart, especially when the apples are so perfectly arranged. But eventually those apples will wither and die, and so will your business if you're not constantly searching for ways to improve it. Even the most loyal customers will abandon you if your product assortment never changes or if you fail to embrace more efficient ways

270

of doing things. You are your own competition, which is why you need to better yourself all the time.

Please don't misunderstand me. I'm not suggesting that you change your operating practices or toss out all your products every six months—though in some high-tech industries you may have to do exactly that.

Nevertheless, you must be willing to make the innovations necessary to strengthen your business. Your goal, after all, should be to serve customers beyond their highest expectations, while building your revenues and streamlining costs. In my experience, the best way to do this is by introducing new products and services and using technology to your maximum advantage.

Industry-leading companies give their customers a reason to buy from them again. Service and quality certainly contribute to this repeat business. But a third variable is that customers walk in expecting to find something new and better on their return trip. In the retail business, Target does an excellent job of playing to this desire. The chain turns its merchandise over quicker than any other discounter, and it is constantly introducing new products, including designer collections that are available for only a limited time.

In what should be the mundane world of home cleaning products and office supplies, 3M is always introducing new and innovative items, including adhesive bandages, scouring pads, air filters, Scotch tape, and Post-it notes. Innovation is such a part of 3M's brand identity—and has been for more than 100 years—the company can truthfully make the claim that people worldwide look to its products to solve problems and make their lives easier and better.

> *You must be willing to make the innovations necessary to strengthen your business.*

Build-A-Bear Workshop also excels at product innovation. We carry, on average, 35 plush animals and 200 outfits, accessories, and shoes at a time, but that mix is constantly changing, driven by the seasons, current events, and changes in fashion. We introduce a new animal every month, and get new clothing items in weekly. We also change the look of our stores 11 times a year. This ensures that our locations always look fresh and that Guests see something new every time they visit us.

Guests know that certain animals and outfits will be available for only a limited time, and this drives sales of these items. In fact, we have some Guests who come in for every product launch so they can add it to their Build-A-Bear collection.

As we innovate, we're careful to balance the newer novelty items with our popular old standards. There are certain bears and outfits that you'll find in all our stores year-round. They are our best-selling items, those that Guests expect us to always carry. I think it's important to keep familiar favorites in your inventory, even as you add products and innovate in other areas.

Innovation isn't just the purview of the research and development department. Continuous improvement should be a company-wide priority.

> *Introducing new products and services gives customers a reason to keep buying from you again and again.*

I suspect that many executives know they're doing some things the hard way within their companies and badly need to upgrade certain systems. But they're reticent to innovate because doing so may cost money, require employee training, or necessitate staffing changes. Still, it's much easier to address inefficiencies and face up to these challenges than to rescue an outmoded, stagnating company whose customers have defected to the competition.

It's very important to keep your computer systems up to date, regardless of what industry you're in. I know this is a constant battle, given all the ongoing innovations that computer manufacturers and software companies make. You should budget proactively for these upgrades because you will need them—probably sooner than you think.

Last year, we rolled out new point-of-sale and merchandising systems at considerable expense. We had to train all our associates on how to use the new systems. There was a huge learning curve and period of adjustment as we installed the new systems in our stores. In the end, however, undertaking this innovation was proven to be the right decision. This new software, in conjunction with our existing purchasing and inventory-control system, has helped us to streamline operations and we're better able to get our most popular products in the right stores at the right time to match customer demand.

> *Continuous improvement should be a company-wide priority.*

I don't know of any business where constant change isn't necessary. Make innovation your company's philosophy and an emblem of your brand, just as it is for 3M.

Let me leave you with several questions to ask yourself in order to spur innovation and improvement within your business.

What products are missing from my inventory?
What can be done to improve my existing products?
Which items would make my customers' lives better?
What changes would make my employees' lives easier?
How can I make the business operate more smoothly?
What changes would increase revenues?
What technology would reduce my costs?
What am I doing the hard way?
What's the easy way?

Speak in All Languages

An amazing thing happened in May 2003. That's when Build-A-Bear Workshop crossed the border into Canada and opened our first international store in Edmonton, Alberta. Six months later, we became a true global brand after opening a store in Sheffield in the United Kingdom.

We now have more than two dozen international locations outside of the United States in Australia, Canada, Denmark, France, Japan, the Netherlands, South Korea, Sweden, Taiwan, and the United Kingdom.

Though I'd always intended to open Build-A-Bear Workshop stores in other countries, our international expansion came much sooner that I initially anticipated because it was clear that the world marketplace was ready for us. As you already know, we copiously track our Guests, using data collected in our stores and from those who register on our web site. That information told us that there was a tremendous international audience for our products.

> *Make your first global forays into countries with demographics, cultures, and languages that are similar to your own.*

By the time we opened in Canada, we had hosted more than 20,000 Canadian visitors in our U.S. stores. When our first location opened in the United Kingdom, we already had a list of more than 30,000 British citizens who had bought from us in places like Orlando, Myrtle Beach, and other U.S. tourist destinations.

Clearly, the world was ready for Build-A-Bear Workshop, and we were ready to take on this global opportunity.

We smartly recognized that we'd have to translate the company for each new international marketplace and that we'd need help doing it.

Every Build-A-Bear Workshop store in the United States is corporately owned. To grow in international markets, however, we embraced a franchise model and selected experienced retail partners to help us launch our brand overseas. We are quite choosy about our franchisees because we give them a tremendous amount of responsibility and autonomy to operate stores in their home countries. We expect our international franchisees to bring experience, sufficient financial backing, deep knowledge of the local marketplace, and passion to the table.

> *Not every business translates well internationally.*

Though I was convinced that kids around the world would respond to our brand, we approached our global expansion very prudently. Most importantly, we made our first international forays into countries that were very similar to the United States, in terms of demographics, language, the economy, spending habits, and family culture. Later, as we ventured into non-English-speaking countries, we chose only those markets with strong consumer economies and large populations of our core audience.

As we've opened stores in places like London, Taipei, Paris, and Tokyo, we've done our best to assimilate to the local culture, while still keeping true to the Build-A-Bear Workshop brand. You'll find outfits and animals in our international stores that you can't find at our locations in the United States. For example, we celebrate the Chinese New Year with the annual introduction of a new animal. In the Year of the Dog, 2006, we introduced a special canine; in 2004, the Year of the Rooster, kids could make and dress their own cock-a-doodle-doo friends. In Japan, we sell traditional kimonos, along with our other clothing. In England, we stock more soccer uniforms and accessories than baseball gear.

Not every business translates well internationally, but I knew that teddy bears had universal appeal. As we like to say, a hug is understood in any language. If your company is rooted in the United States—or even geared to a more narrow local market—you can still learn from my international experience.

The world itself is becoming more homogeneous. Chances are you'll be dealing with vendors from beyond the borders of North America. You need to learn their local cultural and business customs in order to make the relationship work. (In Japan, for instance, be careful not to simply stuff someone's business card into your pocket without looking at it. You're supposed to examine the card when you receive it, treating it with reverence.)

Assimilate your company's operations to the local culture.

If you sell over the Internet, I guarantee you'll receive product inquiries and purchases from other countries. You need to know how to respond to these. How will you accept payments overseas? How will you ship your products? How will you communicate with someone who speaks a different language?

Even in the United States, it's becoming more important to speak in all languages—literally. This country is growing more ethnically diverse with each passing year, and you must be prepared to deal with customers and employees who come from various cultures, and therefore have different customs and celebrate varied religious holidays. Make it easy for those who speak a language other than English to do business with you. Recognizing that our customer base is diverse, we hire bilingual staff in those markets where it's necessary—and the number of such markets increases daily. We also have brochures and other collateral material written in many languages, explaining to Guests of all cultures what Build-A-Bear Workshop is about.

> *Even if you don't expand beyond your own borders, you may still need to serve an ethnically diverse group of customers.*

Beyond that, here are some other lessons I'd like to share with you based on what we've learned from doing business internationally:

- *Choose your partners carefully.* When you hand over responsibility or management of your company to someone else, select partners who are knowledgeable and experienced, and share your passion and vision.
- *Think locally.* As much as possible, tailor your products and services to the local marketplace, while maintaining your brand image.

- *Let your customers be your guides.* Find out where your best customers live and listen to their suggestions when considering a new location or an expansion.

The opportunities to expand your business globally have never been greater. Take the right steps now to ensure your company's products and services will translate well into any language.

Turn "No" into Your Own "Yes"

How many times have you walked into a business and gotten "no" for an answer?

Unfortunately, it happens all the time. Because so many companies fail to give their employees the autonomy to say "yes," "no" has become an acceptable answer in many businesses. Not at Build-A-Bear Workshop. We like to surprise our Guests by saying "yes" as often as we can. In fact, once you embrace this mind-set, it's easier to say "yes" than "no." And it definitely improves your sales.

> *Give employees the privilege of saying "yes" to your customers.*

The following is an elementary example, but it illustrates the point.

A woman walks into a convenience store looking for a late-night snack.

"Do you have any popcorn?" she asks the clerk at the register.

"No," the clerk replies. At the same moment the customer spots a bag of what appears to be white cheddar popcorn across the store.

That convenience store clerk has made two big mistakes. The first is obvious: She isn't familiar with the merchandise in the store. But her second mistake is more unforgivable: The clerk doesn't care about helping the customer.

The clerk could have offered the woman an alternative snack to satisfy her midnight craving, just by asking a few questions. "Do you want something crunchy? We have Rice Krispies Treats. Or how about a box of Cracker Jack? That's popcorn and peanuts. Or if you're looking for something salty, we have pretzels and a lot of different chips."

> *If you don't have the exact product or service a customer wants, find other ways to meet their needs.*

For that sales clerk, the easiest answer is "no." In her mind, her job is simply to ring up the customer's purchases. She isn't empowered to make a sale, and she hasn't been trained in how to make the store's assortment of merchandise more attractive to customers.

She missed a clear "yes" moment. And that's a surefire way to drive customers away.

If you don't offer the exact product or service a customer wants, don't give up on winning that business. Explore other ways you can help the customer. Your alternative may fit his or her needs better than what he or she asked for in the first place.

Even when the obvious answer is "no," that's not always right.

At Build-A-Bear Workshop, we often have Guests who come in with specific requests, such as "Do you have an Atlanta Braves uniform?"

Through our partnership with Major League Baseball, we do carry bear-sized uniforms representing most teams, including the Braves. But we don't sell every uniform in all stores. Sometimes, like any retailer, we also sell out of items.

If someone asked for the uniform of a team we didn't have in stock, the Bear Builder associate would be completely correct if he answered "no" to that question. But at Build-A-Bear Workshop, we're a company that turns "no" into "yes."

If I was working with that Guest, I would offer him several answers. The first, of course, would be "Let me check." Because you really can't know what the answer is unless you investigate the question, I'd check in the back room to make absolutely certain there wasn't a stray uniform for the team the Guest wanted in there. I'd also ask the Guest a few questions of my own and offer some alternatives. "Do you have your heart set on that team's uniform? We have other teams. And we have some generic baseball items—balls, gloves, and bats. Or how about a T-shirt with that team's logo on it?"

> *Never forget that time is money for your customers.*

If the Guest didn't like my other suggestions, I wouldn't give up at strike three. I'd offer to find the uniform at another store or on the company web site and have it delivered to his house.

There are many examples of companies that miss out on the opportunity to turn "no" into "yes."

People shop at discount stores for lots of reasons, but primarily to save money. Yet many discounters ignore the fact that for most consumers time is money. Instead, these stores make customers wait in long lines to purchase any items. Isn't it better to say to a customer, "Yes, I can open up another cash register to ring you up," rather than watching him walk out the door empty-handed?

Nordstrom is the ultimate "yes" company. The upscale department store has a legendary return policy. You can take back anything, and Nordstrom will give you a full refund. The item doesn't even need tags on it, and there's no arbitrary 7-day or 30-day time limit. If a customer decides in June she doesn't want something she bought in December, she can take it back, no questions asked.

> *Offer to perform some services without charge.*
> *It will earn you much respect and goodwill.*

Talbots and Chico's are also like that. I can buy something from them on the Internet or through a catalog. If it doesn't fit, I can return it to the store without any hassles. They make it possible for me to shop any way I want. As a result, I'm inclined to do business with these companies more often.

There's a legendary tale from the mid-1970s about a Nordstrom employee who gave a customer a cash refund for some tires, even though the chain has never sold automobile parts. Whether that story is true or not, there's no denying that Nordstrom has mastered the art of wowing its customers by saying "yes" rather than the expected "no." How many other companies do that? Perhaps they should, because Nordstrom has extraordinary loyalty among its customers, not to mention a strong and well-respected brand. The company is also at the top of its game financially.

We haven't given a refund for tires at Build-A-Bear Workshop yet, but we do something that I believe makes an equally big impression on Guests. Often, people will bring in their old but loved teddy bears that are losing their stuffing. They'll ask if we can add some stuffing and sew them up again. We always say "yes," even if they didn't buy the animal from us. When Guests offer to pay us for this service, we won't accept their cash. Why should we? I think we're much more likely to earn their future business and good word of mouth by honoring such an offbeat request. I don't mind giving away a little free stuffing to make someone happy and generate tremendous goodwill for our business.

> *Seek input and suggestions from frontline employees on how you can turn "no" into "yes" more often.*

You should never miss an opportunity to make a customer's day, whether you're selling jet parts, snack food, tires, stuffed animals, or designer clothing. Because, at the heart of it, every business is really selling *itself*.

At Build-A-Bear Workshop, I'm not the expert in turning "no" into "yes." In this business—and every other one, for that matter—the best blueprint for being a "yes" company comes from those associates who interact with Guests every day.

Bosses should engage their employees in these process changes. Frontline workers know better than anyone what matters most to customers and what riles them. If you want to figure out how to turn "no" into "yes" at your company, seek input and suggestions from those in the trenches. Find out what customer requests they commonly receive, especially those they deny, and discover why that's the normal course of business. Then, figure out a way to turn that "no" into a resounding "yes."

The Harder You Work,
the Luckier You Get

In show business, actors always dream of getting that so-called lucky break. When they do, the headlines often boast about how the new star has become an overnight sensation.

I always laugh when I hear such things. That "overnight sensation" probably spent years—or even decades—working in community theater and taking minor television and movie roles. Lucky break? The reality is most successful people create their own good luck through hard work. And lots of it.

Most successful people create their own luck through hard work.

While the event made him a household name, Tiger Woods didn't pick up a golf club for the first time at the 1997 Masters Tournament. He'd been playing since he was a toddler, practicing his game nearly every day and competing in tournaments through middle school, high school, and college.

Jeff Bezos didn't just luck into a good idea when he started Amazon.com in 1995. He graduated summa cum laude from Princeton University, then honed his business chops as vice president of a big New York bank, and later as a senior vice president for a Wall Street hedge fund.

Author James Patterson hasn't always been a fixture on the bestseller list. He started out as an advertising copywriter. His first novel, *The Thomas Berryman Number*, was published in 1976 by Little, Brown after being turned down by more than two dozen publishers. He simultaneously wrote novels and worked in the advertising business for two more decades, rising to chairman of the J. Walter Thompson ad agency while producing a string of national best sellers, originally on the side.

I'm not a newcomer to the retail industry. I worked in this business for 34 years, progressing from management trainee to company president, before "lucking" into Build-A-Bear Workshop.

The truth is, you won't have any luck in business without hard work. We all make our own opportunities with our attitudes and work ethics. And, as my dad used to say, "The harder you work, the luckier you get."

I didn't grow up with many financial advantages. My parents were first-generation Americans, and both worked incredibly hard. Mom was a social worker, and Dad was a salesman. We were probably the poorest people on our block, yet I never felt that way because we were rich in the ways that mattered. We loved each other very much. We had lots of really good friends, who felt more like family because they'd do anything for us—and we'd do anything for them. We didn't let money, or a lack of it, get in the way of our dreams. I wasn't "lucky" enough to have parents who could afford to spend thousands of dollars on sending me to college. But that didn't mean I didn't get a good education. There was never a doubt in my mind that I'd earn a degree. My lack of financial resources simply meant that I had to work harder and earn better grades to win a scholarship and/or get a job so I could pay my own bills. And that's exactly what I did. I created my own luck.

> *Stop waiting for your lucky break to come.*

As I look back over my life, particularly in relation to Build-A-Bear Workshop, I've been "lucky" on many occasions. Remember the story about how I got my first investor because he read about me in the newspaper? That's all true, and I admit it does seem a bit lucky. But there was plenty of hard work behind that stroke of good fortune. I'd worked on building up my experience in the retail industry and making a name and a reputation for myself in the Saint Louis business community for more than two decades before that. I did my homework in planning the new business, had an airtight business plan, and sold the reporter on doing a story about my company, which subsequently attracted lots of attention.

> *I'm living proof of how "lucky" you can get when you work really hard.*

A few years later, Build-A-Bear Workshop was "lucky" enough to be chosen to have a float in the Macy's Thanksgiving Day Parade. If I hadn't proven myself in business and turned Build-A-Bear Workshop into a nationally recognized brand, we wouldn't have been invited to participate. We designed our float around the 100th anniversary of the teddy bear, and had already been working hard on that marketing effort for some three years. Being part of the parade was truly a tremendous experience and it brought us lots of good fortune. We received national television exposure at a fraction of what a commercial would have cost, and that meant lots of new families learned about our brand. We were fortunate, yes, but we weren't lucky. We worked hard.

I just can't say it any better than my Dad: "The harder you work, the luckier you get." So stop sitting around, waiting for your lucky break to come. Create your own luck! It's what I did. And I'm living proof of just how "lucky" you can get when you work really, really hard.

A few years ago, we hired an outside consulting firm to evaluate future business opportunities and expansion potential for our company. The Parthenon Group out of Boston was a great partner. One big thing they showed us was that while the people who knew us loved us, there were still millions of potential Guests to reach. We then hired the marketing and advertising agency Barkley Evergreen & Partners in Kansas City to partner with our in-house strategic planning team led by Dorrie Krueger, our Managing Director of Strategic Planning, and our talented and tenacious Chief Marketing Bear, Teresa Kroll, to help us learn how to better leverage and serve our Guests. Jeff Fromm, the firm's senior strategist, is an experienced expert on the subject of taking your company to the next level. You can apply the same disciplined thinking to your business by asking the following five questions:

1. What business are you in?
2. Whom do you *really* compete with?

3. Can you dominate the competition based on your sustainable advantage?
4. What are your listening posts?
5. What do you measure, and how quickly will you adjust.

What Business Are You In?

The answer may seem obvious, but it rarely is. Rephrase the question to address what your customers are *really* buying from you, rather than holding to the perspective of what you are trying to sell them. Furthermore, you need to be sure not to answer based on what you *think* customers are looking for, but rather on what you *know* they want through conducting either formal or informal research.

> *You need to probe to discover what your company is all about.*

Formal research involves creating both qualitative and quantitative research measures that help you to understand the components of your value proposition. You then test these components among customers to validate your findings. Putting together effective tests can be tricky, and sometimes it makes sense to bring in outside help to assist with this.

An example of informal research is to talk with a handful of customers, frontline employees, and managers and ask them why customers use your products and services. Be sure to ask follow-up questions if the answers seem a little too obvious.

Using Build-A-Bear Workshop as an example, your inclination might be to say that we're "in the business of selling plush animals to children." We knew that wasn't the case. We're really in the business of letting Guests feel like a kid through self-expression. In a word, we are in the "fun" business. If this wasn't the answer you expected, it shows how important it is to really probe to understand the truth of what your company is all about.

Whom Do You *Really* Compete With?

Regardless of what business you're in, recognize that you have both direct and indirect competition. Rarely are both equally important.

In the case of Build-A-Bear Workshop, there are direct competitors, such as toy stores, but they aren't our real competition. Instead, we need to be concerned about the enormous number of indirect alternatives vying for our Guests' time. Examples include everything from restaurants and skating rinks to movie theaters and zoos.

> *To overshadow the competition, provide a more optimal customer solution.*

Being able to see with whom and with what you really compete often isn't easy. In many cases, you will see only the direct competition, which certainly should not be ignored. Above all, it's critical to understand how you can provide a more optimal customer solution, in order to outflank the competition and win over the hearts of consumers.

Can You Dominate the Competition Based on Your Sustainable Advantage?

Don't subscribe to just one theory of competition. Look at every situation and apply a multitude of unique tools to ensure that you consider as many alternatives as possible. This brings us back to a concept first introduced in the chapter in Part Four entitled "The Five Pillars of Success."

As a reminder, these pillars are price, convenience, product innovation, customer service, and the overall experience. Using this model, your company must maintain at least a threshold level of excellence, or what Jeff Fromm calls the cost of entry, on all five pillars. The critical ingredient is for you to dominate your competition on at least one of the pillars in a way that is meaningful to your customers.

Being great at all five pillars is unrealistic. Narrow your focus and dominate those that are meaningful to your company, that will give you a sustainable advantage, and that you know will be highly rewarded by loyal customers.

What Are Your Listening Posts?

Listening posts can be either formal or informal ways of gaining insights from customers. The goal is to segment customers in such a way that you can identify the key drivers for each one.

> *Use listening posts to gain insights from your customers.*

Do you think a five-year-old girl has the same drivers (or motivations) for coming to a Build-A-Bear Workshop store as a 12-year-old girl? Of course not. The two are at very different stages of development. The five-year-old craves tactile experiences, while the 12-year-old is entering her teenage years and is likely to be more focused on self-expression. We frequently get better information from our younger Guests by talking to our store associates or through conducting parent/child interviews. For the older kids, however, it's often beneficial to conduct "friends" interviews, where we speak with two or three girls at the same time to get their collective thoughts.

Your listening posts could be your store managers, customer service agents (these are an especially great source of information and insights), or even the company receptionist. With e-mail, it's possible to be in contact with some segment of your best customers on an ongoing basis, as we are.

The bottom line is that you will benefit from having multiple and, where possible, real-time sources of feedback. Much of the information you get will come to you filtered. By having multiple sources, you are in a prime position to get more and better data to inform your decisions.

What Do You Measure, and How Quickly Will You Adjust?

Every company closely tracks its sales, profits, gross margins, and various other traditional monetary data points. While all of these are critically important business metrics, they are simply not enough because they deal with only what Jeff calls the "rearview mirror."

> *Getting information from multiple sources will give you more data to make better decisions.*

What does your *future* look like, and how can you shape it? To answer that, you need more information than what is probably already at your immediate disposal.

The following are some areas you need to get a better understanding of in order to pave the path for a prosperous future for your business:

- What is the unaided awareness of your brand? (The more, the better.)
- How is your brand perceived? (If it's not seen as *the* industry leader, you've got work to do.)
- How loyal are your customers? (Loyal customers are the only kind to have.)
- Are they highly satisfied? (Note that merely satisfied customers aren't loyal at all.)

- What is the lifetime value of a highly satisfied, loyal customer? (In a word, loyal customers are priceless.)
- Are you getting great word-of-mouth referrals from your loyal customers? (If not, why not?)

You should make ongoing tweaks in how you do business to make sure what you are doing is working to develop this incredible customer loyalty. It's something we are constantly aware of at Build-A-Bear Workshop, and together our outside agency and internal marketing team keep it at the forefront of everything we do.

Having a process in place for learning and then acting on the answers to these five questions is bound to put you miles ahead of the competition for years to come.

Part Seven

Giving Back

Good Works Are
Good Business

Much of this book thus far has dealt with strategies for achieving the personal and professional success you most desire for yourself. In this closing section, I want to talk briefly about the importance of sharing part of your prosperity in business with others—especially those who are less fortunate than you.

My mother worked very hard as a social worker, yet never made much money. That meant her own life was tougher than it should have been. But I don't believe Mom would have been happy doing any other kind of work. She lived to help others; it made her heart beat.

It's not how much money you make that defines your success, but rather what impact you have on the world.

Mom always taught me that no matter how hard you think your life is, there are others who are worse off. It is, therefore, our moral duty to help other people, she said. Mom, more than anyone I've encountered before or since, practiced what she preached. She was always doing for others, often more than she did for herself.

I'm thankful to have had such a role model. I learned very early on that it's not how much money you make that defines your success, but rather what impact you have on the world.

I enjoy giving back, both as an individual and as a business executive. I'm never happier than when I'm helping someone, realizing that my actions have made someone else's life better.

In my opinion, philanthropy, whether through monetary donations or the gift of your time and expertise, is an essential personal moral imperative. It's also increasingly becoming crucial to the wellbeing of your business.

I think it's important for companies to have a heart and to contribute. In a sense, it's a way of paying back the universe for our own good fortune.

Throughout my professional career, and especially since founding Build-A-Bear Workshop, I've made philanthropy a priority. Giving back to others, especially within the communities in which we operate, is a primary principle on which this company is built.

> *Contributing to others is a way of paying back the universe for your own good fortune.*

Consumers have many choices in how and where to spend their money. Many choose to support socially responsible companies that help causes they are passionate about. More and more companies are starting to see the connection between doing good and having a prosperous business. Your charitable work shouldn't be motivated by what you'll get out of it, but it is a nice side benefit to know that good works can make your business stronger. To paraphrase the Good Book, give and it shall be given back to you.

We've focused our charitable efforts on those causes that matter most to our Guests and their families, especially those causes that benefit children. We've also found ways to involve *them* in the philanthropy.

We have several special animals—Nikki's Bear, Bearemy's Kennel Pals friends, and Read Teddy—that are associated with specific causes and charities. Whenever a Guest buys one of these lovable creatures, we make a donation to that cause.

We recently introduced our third Nikki's Bear, which is named for 14-year-old Nikki Giampolo. Nikki loved life, children, and teddy bears. She shared that love by giving bears and hugs to all those around her. Sadly, Nikki lost her life to cancer in 2002. But her courage and spirit live on. Nikki's mom and friends shared her story of hope with us. Her good works inspired us to create Nikki's Bear in order to help other children with cancer. A portion of the proceeds from the sale of all Nikki's Bears is distributed through the Build-A-Bear Workshop Foundation to fund children's health and wellness programs.

Meanwhile, proceeds from the sales of Bearemy's Kennel Pals friends benefit animal welfare organizations, and Read Teddy raises money for children's literacy. We also have a series of World Wildlife Fund animals, and those sales support efforts to protect endangered animals and their habitats.

In 2001, we started a very special program called Stuffed With Hugs. We were inspired by the selfless efforts of our caring Guests. Often, our store managers would share stories about kids who had raised money or saved their allowances so they could make stuffed animals for other children in need. We decided to embrace this idea in a big way. Every May, we hold Stuffed With Hugs events in all our stores. We let Guests come to our stores and make bears for free that are then donated to a good cause. In 2005, we partnered with UNICEF to distribute the Stuffed With Hugs animals to children affected by the Asian tsunami.

We also have a Stuffed With Hugs event in conjunction with every store grand opening. Since the program started, we've donated more than 150,000 bears to children in troubled situations.

This practice of partnering with our Guests in philanthropy is what's known as *cause marketing*. We're able to do good things for worthy causes, while also making an emotional connection with our Guests and positioning Build-A-Bear Workshop as a company that cares.

> *The practice of partnering with your customers in philanthropy is what's known as* cause marketing.

American Express essentially pioneered cause marketing in 1983. It was the first company to involve customers in a philanthropic effort when it pledged to donate money from each American Express card purchase a customer made to a fund earmarked to restoring the Statue of Liberty.

Lee Jeans is another company that has successfully linked its brand with a cause. In 1996, motivated in part by the impact breast cancer had on the lives of people they knew, the company's executives decided to sponsor Lee National Denim Day to raise money for breast cancer research. The idea was quite simple: In exchange for a $5 donation to the Susan G. Komen Breast Cancer Foundation, employees got to wear jeans to work one Friday in October.

In the first year, about 4,000 companies participated in National Denim Day. Now, some 28,000 businesses do. Since 1996, Lee National Denim Day has raised more than $52 million for breast cancer research, education, screening, and treatment programs.

The event has been successful both in raising money for the foundation and in solidifying Lee's reputation as a company with a heart. What's the recipe for success? The fund-raiser emphasizes

Lee's core product—jeans—and a cause that is important to its core customer base—women.

You can always write a check to a charity—and we do that, too. But when you get your customers and associates involved in both the fund-raising and the cause, it makes a much stronger statement about the kind of company you are. And it has a more lasting impact on consumer perceptions. It gives people yet another reason to do business with you.

> *When you get your customers involved in both the fund-raising and the cause, it makes a much stronger statement about the kind of company you are.*

Think about the ways you can give back in your company. Doing so will not only make you feel better, it will make your customers feel better about you.

When you weave the spirit of giving and community responsibility into the DNA of your company, the rewards are immeasurable.

As the old saying goes, charity does begin at home—and you need look no further than your own backyard to find good causes to support.

We're a national company, and we've given quite a bit of financial support and merchandise over the years to national causes. But when it comes to philanthropy, our priority has always been to tend to local needs first.

> *When it comes to philanthropy, our priority is to support local needs first.*

In the beginning, when we just had stores in Missouri, that meant focusing solely on charities and causes within that state's borders. Now that we have locations around the world, our definition of *local* has broadened. Still, whenever we have a fund-raising event at one of our stores, we try to keep the money in that particular community.

With a few special exceptions, like the Asian tsunami and Hurricane Katrina, bears made during our annual Stuffed With Hugs events and grand opening "cele-bear-ations" are donated to local kids in need. Sometimes, the animals are given to a local children's hospital or orphanage, or to the American Red Cross, which passes them out to kids whose homes are destroyed by fire or other disasters. Our Bearemy's Kennel Pals program, while national in scope, is local in its reach. Proceeds are distributed to domestic pet programs in those communities where we have stores.

We're all citizens of the world, and I think it's our responsibility to make it a better place, beginning right where we live. That's a responsibility we all share as individual and corporate citizens.

> *It's our responsibility to make the world a better place, beginning right where we live.*

To demonstrate the commitment of Build-A-Bear Workshop to local charities, we started our Huggable Heroes program in 2004. Like Nikki's Bears, this program was inspired by Nikki Giampolo. We launched a search in 2004 to find other children and teenagers like Nikki who were doing something special for their community and the people in it. Huggable Heroes, like Nikki, are special people who do things both big and small.

As with any contest, we had to pick a list of winners from all the Huggable Heroes entries we received. We eventually narrowed the field to 10 individual and 5 group winners, and made donations to charities that those Huggable Heroes support. Our goal was to encourage the local charitable work of each of the Huggable Heroes recipients and to encourage children to become involved in causes in their own neighborhoods. We selected a semifinalist from each participating Build-A-Bear Workshop store and awarded each of them with a $35 gift certificate.

I was personally inspired by the work and activism of our Huggable Heroes. I can't share all their stories here, but I will tell you about a few of them.

Shannon, for one, has volunteered to help out at dozens of leading adult and youth literacy and education programs. Her passion for philanthropy began at age 8 when she took the llamas her family raises to nursing homes to interact with elderly residents. Now 16, Shannon has led a variety of outdoor workshops to teach kids about wildlife, and she organizes monthly themed parties at the local public library to introduce youngsters to the fun of reading.

Another teen, Brooke, regularly works with the Toys for Tots program by singing in toy stores while the Marines collect donations. When the Marines told Brooke that they constantly ran short of gifts for teens, she was motivated to act. With the approval of the local Marine Corps Reserves, Brooke founded Toys for Teens and began collecting gifts and money for underprivileged teens. Nearly 3,000 teens have received holiday gifts as a result of Brooke's efforts.

After visiting an inner-city elementary school library in West Michigan two years ago, Jennifer realized that she probably had more books at home than the small school library had on its shelves. So, she organized a fund-raising campaign called Dream Reading. To date, Jennifer has raised $15,000 to buy books for inner-city school libraries, receiving donations from her local community and across the country.

Zachary, another Huggable Hero, has rescued more than 200 homeless pets and found homes for more than half of them so far. In 2003, with help from family and friends, Zachary created Parents Involved in Education (PIE). The group makes presentations at schools, libraries, and community groups to raise awareness and funds for the support and expansion of a no-kill animal shelter, pet rescue service, and wellness clinic called Friendz for Life Sanctuary. In 2004, nearly $7,000 was raised because of Zachary's efforts.

Each of the Huggable Heroes proves that a single person can make a difference and that they can do so where they live. They've strengthened my own resolve to give back and focus the philanthropy of Build-A-Bear Workshop locally where it can make the most difference in the lives of our associates and Guests.

That's the approach every company should take regarding charity. Start by giving locally, where your donation can benefit those who work for and support your business.

That being said, it's good to have global ambitions. I recently had the opportunity to share a life-changing experience with a team of Build-A-Bear Workshop associates. We were given a chance to create a small version of one of our stores for a day for children in South Africa who had been orphaned by AIDS. We live in such a safe environment in the United States where AIDS is under control and never was the epidemic for children that it is in Africa.

Most of these children are innocent victims whose parents died of AIDS and passed on the disease to their children in the womb. In the cases of other young girls and boys, they contracted AIDS through rape or a violent crime.

For almost all of these children, whether they were 3 or 23, this was the first time they had ever owned a stuffed animal, let alone one they made themselves. The smiles on their faces the day they met us didn't tell you much about their painful past, but it did foretell hope for their future. They are strong, motivated, and anxious to change the world. We were honored to share our hugs with these special, loving kids. Little did they know that they also changed our lives forever.

The response for volunteers among associates for this long-distance project was mind-boggling. Even though this meant time away from their own families, arduous travel, and long work hours, many offered to pay their own way. That was really no surprise to me, because that's what the human teddy bears in our company often do. But regardless of how often it happens, it always warms my heart because it is above and beyond what is expected of their jobs.

I hope you find a way to put this true spirit of giving in your company as well.

Share and Share Alike

As I'm sure you've gathered by now, I have encountered many people throughout my life who have invested in the successes I enjoy today.

My mom. My dad. Family friends. My teachers. My college professors. My husband. My friends. Stanley Goodman (the former CEO at the May Department Stores). My investors.

So many have helped me along the way, I feel obliged to return their generosity. One way I do that is by helping others—both kids and aspiring adult entrepreneurs—to make their own dreams come true. And when they do, I hope they'll perpetuate the goodwill by helping others to do the same.

I wouldn't be where I am today without help.

It can get pretty busy, not to mention hectic and stressful, when you're running a company. It would be easy to brush off someone's

307

request for help or advice with a curt "I'm too busy." But I always try to make the time to share my experience and advice with anyone who sincerely asks for help. Because of my willingness to lend a hand, I probably don't get enough sleep or take enough free time for myself, but those things seem less important than helping others to succeed.

I know I wouldn't be where I am today without help. Remember, it takes a village to raise a bear. I still recall everyone who took the time to answer my questions and explain the workings of business to me. Advice from mentors was enormously beneficial.

That's the main reason I decided to write this book. Yes, I was excited to share the story of Build-A-Bear Workshop. More importantly, I wanted to pass on to other current and aspiring entrepreneurs all of the knowledge I have been blessed to receive over the years.

In return, I hope you'll remember to take the time to share your knowledge when you become even more successful than you are today. No one sets out to be a mentor, but we all have the chance to be one when we take a few moments to teach and help others to improve their skills.

As a businessperson, you have many opportunities to share your knowledge and assist others with their careers. Sometimes, it may be as easy as answering an e-mail. I receive inquiries all the time from kids, and sometimes even adults, who are working on school papers and want to ask a few questions about my company and career. I always oblige.

> *We all have a chance to be a mentor when we take a few moments to teach and help others to improve their skills.*

I also speak frequently at college campuses, usually once a month, and personally support the John M. Olin School of Business at Washington University in Saint Louis. One of my favorite speaking gigs is talking to students enrolled in the school's retailing class.

That transports me back to my own days at the University of Georgia when I was on the other side of the desk listening to Dr. Carter's lectures, which sparked my interest in retailing. I hope I can do the same for other students.

Each summer, we hire a dozen or so interns and put them to work in real jobs within the company. They work hard, but they also learn a lot, as I did in my internships and management trainee positions.

I've also recently begun investing my own money in other people's business ideas. Certainly, I hope for a return on my investment, but profit isn't my primary motivation. I like the idea of being an angel investor. It's a bit like being a fairy godmother. You have the power to help make someone's dream come true. And it feels good to play that role. That's really all the return I need to feel fulfilled.

> *You have the power to help make someone else's dream come true.*

When I needed advice, help, and money, I was so grateful to those willing to give it to me. Now, it's my turn to be on the giving side. As one of my most favorite Bearisms teaches, it is better to gift than to receive.

I certainly hope my gift to you of this book has inspired your imagination and showed you how to achieve your highest goals in business. I look forward to hearing more about your successes and know that many great things are in store for your future.

Bearisms to Live and Work By

Following are some of the fun sayings we have come up with at Build-A-Bear Workshop that guide how we do business. Sure, they're cute and often a bit goofy. Some are as sweet and sugary as honey. Nevertheless, they contain a lot of truths that businesspeople of all ages can surely benefit from.

Enjoy the simple truths contained in these Bearisms, which remind us of some golden, but often overlooked, rules that, when followed, are sure to lead to a better life—and more prosperity in your chosen profession.

A bear hug is understood in any language.
A bear hug is worth a thousand words.
A bear's smile is contagious.
A bear will walk a mile fur a friend.
A day without honey is unbearable!
A friend is a present you give yourself.
A little bear hug makes a big difference.
Always bee kind.
Always give the good stuff.
Always put your best paw forward.
Ask not what your bear can do fur you, but what you can do fur
    your bear.
A smile is the best a bear can wear.
A stitch in time saves patches.
A teddy is a present you give yourself.
Bear in mind: Always be kind.
Bears are measured by the size of their heart.
Bears count their blessings one friend at a time.

Bears teach you to love one hug at a time.
Bears who are loved are bears in luck.
Bear your heart.
Beauty is in the eye of the bearholder.
Be kind. Be true. Bee honey.
Be pawsitive.
Be the bearer of good news.
Big or small, always cele-bear-ate your accomplishments.
Don't fur-get to lend your paw to a friend in need.
Don't judge a bee by its buzz.
Don't worry—be furry.
Everyone has a soft spot.
Everything is pawsible when you put your mind to it.
Friendship is a gift fur all seasons.
Furry or fuzzy, a hug is always beary nice.
Go fur it!
Great bears come in many sizes.
Honey is meant to be gulped, not sipped.
Honey tastes better when you share it with a friend.
Hugs are beary essential.
If it's meant to bee, it's up to me.
I never met a teddy I didn't like.
It's better to gift than to receive.
It's okay to let your stuffing show.
It's never too late to have a happy childhood.
It's not the size of the bear that counts; it's the size of its heart!
It takes a village to raise a bear.
Just Hug!
Libearty fur all.
Life is always sweeter with a little honey.
Live simply, love well and take time to taste the honey along the
    way.
Love is The Stuff Inside.
Never bear a grudge.
Nothing tops a bear hug—it's the bee's knees!

One small step for bears, one giant leap for bearkind.
Pawsitive stuff happens one paw at a time.
Paws were made fur helping.
Reach fur the stars.
Remembear: Inside is the best of me—real heart determines my
  destiny.
Remembear the sweets in life: friends, love, and kindness.
Remembear your very first teddy.
Take heart—the best is yet to bee.
Take time to paws for thought.
Take time to taste the honey.
The fur may fade but friendship lasts furever.
The good stuff is the stuff inside.
There are no limits when bears put their minds to it.
There is always a reason to paw-ty!
There is no friend like an old friend.
The world is a stage and every bear plays its part.
Think like a bear of action, act like a bear of thought.
True friends bear your faults.
True friends share stuff.
When friends hug, hearts warm.
When some teddy loves you, you're someone special.
You aren't born a bear, you become a bear.
You're all fluff unless you nurture your heart stuff.

Acknowledgments

From Maxine Clark:

One of the best parts of creating Build-A-Bear Workshop is the thousands of Guests around the world who have connected with us, been proud of our accomplishments, become our friends, and encouraged me to write this book. I've had a very successful 30-plus-year career in retailing doing what I love—interpreting trends and turning them into profitable businesses. Most of these years were spent with the May Department Stores Company learning from retailing giants like Stanley Goodman, Allan Bloostein, David Farrell, Ken Kolker, and Julie Seeherman. While I didn't invent teddy bears or factories that make them, I did take the idea of making your own stuffed animals to a different level by giving it a heart and a soul—the vital ingredients that are necessary to turn a business concept into an enduring brand.

They say the best homage you can pay to your teachers is to pass it on. So when the requests for business help came pouring in, I decided a book might be the perfect way to share what I have learned and what I think is possible to achieve in any business. For me, the retail business has been like being paid to do my hobby, and I hope that you, my readers, will see the opportunity to take what you love and turn it into a highly profitable way to make a living.

At Build-A-Bear Workshop we like to say that "it takes a village to raise a bear." The same is true for this author. So many people have contributed to my success in life and, in many ways, in turn helped me write this book.

To Katie and Jack Burkhardt (and bears George and Teddy), whose greatest contribution to me as a person is their willingness to let me be a kid in their presence and never think it is silly or odd (well, at least they never said so out loud so I would hear it!), thanks, guys. You are truly my inspiration for staying a kid *always*. I know you both have aspirations of your own, and while I would love for retailing to wear off on you, I just want you to love what you do—as ultimately that will bring you the most happiness and success. Elaine and Steve, thanks for generously sharing your kids and your friendship with me!

I always loved school and I can remember every teacher I have ever had, but a few stand out and remain my silent coaches even today. Mrs. Grace, my first grade teacher, taught me not only to take risks, but also to learn from them and then take new risks. Mr. George Vasquez, my fifth grade teacher, taught me to love the science of problem solving. Mr. Jeff Rosinek (now Judge Rosinek), my high school government teacher, and Mrs. Marlene Adams, my high school journalism teacher, encouraged my sense of community, the importance of standing up for my beliefs, and being able to communicate those passions and visions to others.

To Dr. Robert Carter, my college marketing professor: thank you, thank you, thank you for getting to know me not just as a student but as a young person with hopes and dreams and encouraging me to consider a career in retailing. I am forever indebted to you and I hope you can see that the lessons you taught me are alive and well at Build-A-Bear Workshop.

To my parents, Ken and Anne Kasselman, thank you for encouraging me to be an independent person accountable for my own choices and, yes, for encouraging me to see things through rose-colored glasses—the world is full of rosy possibilities if you let yourself dream. Mom, you were a great role model for me as a career woman and, importantly, as a generous person. While I did not always appreciate your selfless dedication to your passion (kids with Down syndrome), I do understand it today and I treasure all that you taught me about sharing with others and making a difference.

To Barney Ebsworth and Wayne Smith for believing in me before there was a store and making it possible through your financial partnership. To Mark Zorensky, Jimmy Gould, Bill Reisler, and Frank Vest and all of my partners, your investment and support have allowed so many kids to smile around the world. And Adrienne Weiss—thanks for helping bring this brand to life. I hope you are as proud of what we have created as I am.

To our landlords, thanks for your faith in what I am sure seemed like a long shot. You have been a vital part of our success, and I value your early and continued vision to see the possibilities that Build-A-Bear Workshop would bring to your malls.

To all of the associates of Build-A-Bear Workshop, including our Cub Advisory Board, thanks for inspiring me every day by your passion for what you do and for helping me build this great brand into what it has become and what it will continue to be. You are "pawsome"! Special thanks to Tina Klocke, Marilyn Freundlich, Jill Saunders, and Teresa Kroll, my earliest team members and friends. You are my right and left hand(s) and I am proud to have you has friends and partners.

To Jeff Fromm, Staci Alferman, Kirk Kazanjian, and Amy Joyner, my cohorts in this book writing project. This would never have been possible without your encouragement and talent. I hope that this book we have created together will encourage many aspiring entrepreneurs as well as current business owners to add the needed heart and soul to take their businesses to the next level.

And last, but certainly not least, to my wonderful husband and partner Bob Fox. Thank you for being my best friend, number one cheerleader, and the wind beneath my wings. You have always believed in me and indulged my wild and crazy ideas. Together we have built two great businesses and expanded our family beyond our wildest expectations. We make a great team!

From Amy Joyner:

My biggest thanks go to Maxine Clark, who set aside many mornings and afternoons to share her story with me. Countless other Build-A-Bear Workshop employees have also played a role. I'd like to single out Patty Kious, Jill Saunders, Ronnie Gaubatz, and Carrie Strindel, who shared their expertise and provided me with reams of background material on the company.

I also want to thank Jeff Fromm and Mike Swensen of Barkley Evergreen & Partners and Margaret Bell of In-house Media for their insights on marketing, cause branding, and advertising.

I owe a debt of gratitude to Kirk Kazanjian at Literary Productions and Debra Englander at John Wiley & Sons as well for allowing me to be a part of this project.

Finally, I must mention the friends and family who provided me space, peace, and quiet when I was on deadline and who celebrated with me when I needed a break. Thank you very much, Margaret, Aulica, McCoy, Patrick, Ryan, Koni, Bob, Martha, Grandma, Mom, Dad, and, of course, Bruce.

About the Authors

Maxine Clark is one of the retail industry's true innovators. During a career spanning more than 30 years, she has shown an uncanny ability to spot emerging trends. She founded the innovative retail chain Build-A-Bear Workshop in 1997 and has been the company's Chief Executive Bear ever since. She has also served as chair of the company's board of directors since its conversion to a corporation in April 2000.

Before founding Build-A-Bear Workshop, Clark was president of Payless ShoeSource, and previously spent more than 19 years in various divisions of the May Department Stores Company. Her executive roles over the years have included merchandise development, merchandise planning, merchandise research, marketing, and product development.

There are now more than 200 Build-A-Bear Workshop stores worldwide. In addition to the United States, the company has locations in Canada, Australia, Denmark, France, Japan, the Netherlands, South Korea, Taiwan, and the United Kingdom. Clark's newest addition to the entertainment retail industry is a concept called "friends 2B made," which launched in 2004. Each "friends 2B made" store is built around the simple premise that kids, especially girls, love dolls.

Build-A-Bear Workshop, "friends 2B made," and Clark have been consistently recognized for their achievements in the industry. Build-A-Bear Workshop was a 2005 iParenting Media HOT Award Winner, crowned the 2005 "Portfolio Company of the Year" by the National Association of Small Business Investment Companies, named one of the International Council of Shopping Centers' "Hottest Retailers of 2004," and awarded Retail Innovator of the Year for 2001 by the National Retail Federation. Clark's "friends 2B made" concept received a first place award in the *Chain Store Age* 2004 Retail Store of the Year Design Competition, and she was named a Customer-Centered Leader in the 2005 Customer First Awards by *Fast Company*. Clark was also called one of the Wonder Women of Toys by *Playthings* and was a national retail finalist for the 2004 Ernst & Young Entrepreneur of the Year award. In 2006, she was inducted into the Junior Achievement U.S. Business Hall of Fame.

Clark has been featured in newspapers and magazines around the world, and has appeared as a guest on numerous network and nationally syndicated television shows.

She is a member of the board of directors of the J.C. Penney Company, where she serves as chairman of the Corporate Governance Committee. She is also on the boards of Barnes Jewish Hospital, the Simon Youth Foundation, the International Council of Shopping Centers, Washington University in Saint Louis, and the University of Georgia Foundation at her alma mater. In addition, Clark is chair of Teach for America Saint Louis and a member of the Committee of 200, a leading organization for women entrepreneurs around the world.

She can be reached by e-mail at maxineclark@buildabear.com.

Amy Joyner is an award-winning author and business reporter who has been writing about entrepreneurship for many years. In addition to *The Bear Necessities of Business*, she is the co-author of *Making Dough* and author of *The eBay Millionaire*, both published by John Wiley & Sons.

Joyner is a former business reporter for the *News & Record* in Greensboro, North Carolina. She has received three Knight Center Fellowships for business, aviation security, and military reporting, and won numerous awards for her writing over the years from such organizations as the Associated Press and North Carolina Press Association.

Joyner has been a guest on many radio and TV shows, including CNN, CNBC, the BBC, and National Public Radio. Her work has also been featured in such newspapers and magazines as *Fortune* and the *Washington Post*, which chose *The eBay Millionaire* as its selection of the month for the Color of Money Book Club.

Joyner is a graduate of the University of North Carolina at Chapel Hill and currently lives in Greensboro, North Carolina.

Index

658
Cla   Clark, Maxine K.

        The bear necessi-
        ties of business

                        F606   24.95

DUE DATE

658 CLA
Clark, Maxine K.
The bear necessities of
33292009211453   PA